Circling
——the——
Divine

Circling
——the——
Divine

Spiritual Reflections
for the Journey

R. SCOTT COLGLAZIER

Chalice Press
St. Louis, Missouri

Biblical quotations, unless otherwise noted, are from the New Revised Standard Version Bible, copyright 1989, Division of Christian Education of the National Council of Churches of Christ in the USA. Used by permission.

Cover: Kathi Bell
Interior design: Elizabeth Wright

This book is printed on acid-free, recycled paper.

Visit Chalice Press on the World Wide Web at
www.chalicepress.com

10 9 8 7 6 5 4 3 2 1   98 99 00 01 02 03

Library of Congress Cataloging–in–Publication Data

Colglazier, R. Scott, 1956–
    Circling the divine : spiritual reflections for the journey / by R. Scott Colglazier.
        p.   cm.
    ISBN 0-8272-0473-6
    1. Sermons, American.   I. Title
    BV4253.C65   1998   98–17313
    252—dc21   CIP

Printed in the United States of America

Acknowledgments

There are so many people who have participated, not just in this book, but in my calling as a minister whom I would like to acknowledge.

I want to thank my administrative assistant, Sallie Tomlinson, for all her help and support—not only with this manuscript, but for orchestrating a demanding schedule, keeping time clear for my study and writing, and being the one person who says to me again and again, "Scott, preaching is *the* most important thing you do here."

Special appreciation goes to Rev. Kathy Palen, who brought her editing skills and insights to this manuscript. She has the remarkable gift of understanding the connection between the preached word, the heard word, the written word, and finally the word read off the page. Thank you.

I would like to thank Ron Allen of Christian Theological Seminary, who helped me understand the power and possibilities of preaching and who has continued to take an interest in my preaching. To Clark Williamson, who has helped shape my theological understanding, I offer my word of appreciation. And though we do not really know one another, I think of preachers such as Fred Craddock, Frederick Buechner, Joey Jeter, William Sloane Coffin, Jr., James Forbes, William Willimon, Alvin Jackson, Arthur Calliandro, Barbara Brown Taylor, Susan Bond, and David Buttrick—these and others have helped me understand the beauty and poignancy of preaching.

A special word of gratitude goes to my family. Each Saturday my wife, Marti, takes time to hear my sermon in the kitchen or laundry room or living room. Rarely has any congregation heard a sermon without her sensitive listening. Time and time again she has offered the right critical word or the affirming response. To Matthew, Drew, and Katie, I say thanks for putting up with the weekly pressure I feel as Sunday grows closer. In some ways, this family has helped me understand the challenge and importance of preaching.

For the people at Southport Christian Church in Indianapolis—people such as Chris and Lisa, Jim and Nina, Mike and Patti, Gene and Joan, Jim and Paula, Becky, Rose and Harry, Nick and Ann, and so many others who shaped my life—I say thanks.

For the people at Beargrass Christian Church in Louisville, people I knew briefly, but with depth and great feeling—Ron and Leslie, Jim and Judy, Wayne and Pam, Terry B., Leonard and Ann, Bob and Susan, Doug and Tassie, John and Patti, Frank and Ann, Karen, Chris and Scott, Rick and Susan, Bruce and Becki—all of these and many more have been friends and eager listeners.

And finally, I want to say thank you and dedicate this book to the members of University Christian Church. Though my ministry is still in a beginning stage, I am so grateful to preach to you week after week. This church has had such an awesome tradition of good preaching—one which, when I pause too long to consider it, can become rather intimidating. Yet, each week when I see you in our beautiful Romanesque sanctuary or talk to you after one of our services or overhear you talk in the hallway about a sermon, I am assured again and again that this rather strange process of writing and preaching, unlike any other art form, finally does make a difference. Indeed, we circle the divine together.

Table of Contents

Section IV Edification

Introduction

Not long ago I was talking to a young couple at a party. They were nicely dressed, handsome, showing signs of early success in their respective careers. She was an accountant. He was a doctor. As we talked, the conversation turned to church. It always does! They were telling me about their religious background; how they had gotten away from church in their twenties but now were beginning to attend church again and, in fact, were loving their new church home. I had seen them at my congregation of University Christian Church but had not had a chance to meet them. They seemed so enthusiastic about their new religious connection that I couldn't help but ask them a question: *So, what is it that you hope to get out of going to church?*

I think they were a little surprised that I, their prospective new minister, would ask them such a question. But they responded with some of the most thoughtful remarks I think I've ever heard. They talked about their need to be connected to a community, to have a place where their two children could grow up. They spoke with high hopes of wanting to give something back to the community. And then they said, "To be honest, we like coming to church because we get something out of the sermons." Fascinating. *Get something out of the sermons.*

Nothing, absolutely nothing, in the general culture supports their churchgoing. If this young couple wakes up on Sunday morning, if they go to the trouble of getting dressed and getting their two children dressed, driving to a church building, dropping their children off in a classroom, and then heading to the sanctuary, if all that happens, it happens because there is some internal motivation and connection that has become powerful and meaningful. And though they mentioned a variety of reasons for connecting to the church, it is this unique moment of listening to a sermon that was singled out.

A sermon. There's nothing quite like it, is there? We've all heard them. Some have anesthetized us to the point of slumber. Others have left us indifferent. Still others perhaps have muddied the waters of faith to the point of our exclaiming, "I just didn't get it!" But then there are those rare moments, moments when the right words, the right feelings, the right openness come together, and something clicks inside. A cheering section rises up inside our soul and shouts, "Yes!" And that yes is not just to the sermon or to the oratory of the moment; it is a deeper yes—a yes to the living God.

1

I know that eucharist is important. I would never want to undermine the depth and power of ritual in a worship service. Even the very architecture of a sanctuary tells the story of faith. And yes, musicians and singers, anthems and musical responses are clearly indispensable. But all of those elements can be present in a service, and yet if the sermon is boring or confused or flat or passionless, if the sermon lacks any religious claim on human experience, then the worshiper goes home empty. There is no way to overstate the importance of coming to church and hearing a sermon, a message, an extraordinary moment of communication that helps a person make contact with the living presence of God. That, of course, is the quintessential quality of any sermon—helping people make contact with the divine.

If that is the case, I would suggest that a sermon is not designed primarily to impart information. Imparting information is important, and it is true that some sermons evolve into more of a teaching message. But merely to pass out information about the "Johannine this" or the "Pauline that" is a mistake of the first order. Experience is everything! In fact, the Bible itself can be understood as a compilation of experiences, told and retold, not for history's sake, but to elicit new and present experiences with God. Biblical stories become rooms, not to sit in and admire like a president's restored home, but places to feel again, think again, live again. Therefore, in any sermon there is a need to tell the stories, to share the the ideas and the feelings that finally touch head and heart, intellect and soul, bringing people into an encounter with God. The preaching moment is a moment of circling the divine.

I should quickly add that sermons are a matter of taste. There are some sermons that I don't necessarily care for, but about which others absolutely rave. That seems fair enough. As you read these sermons, you may like some more than others. Fine. The chances of all of them connecting with every reader are slim to none. What I hope as I preach is that at one time or another over the course of several years some of my sermons will connect with all of my listeners, though I know that will never happen on one given Sunday.

What then constitutes a sermon that allows us to soar and circle around God? I would suggest that a sermon first of all needs to be *interesting*. Boring sermons coming from boring ministers constitute an unpardonable sin. A sermon also needs to offer some kind of coherent *theological vision*. What does the sermon say about God? What insight about God is being offered? What dimension of God am I asked to grapple with this week as I listen to the sermon? I would then suggest that a sermon needs to *tell the story*. What story? Partly the story of human experience. It must be real. Genuine. Sincere is not enough. A sermon needs to take some risk and become transparent. This is especially demanding for the preacher. It's like giving birth each week. Some babies are easier than others, but none are a walk in the park! Additionally, a sermon must tell God's story. That's a quality for every sermon. A sermon should be some expression of the *good news of God through Jesus Christ*. A sermon begs for *image and innovation*. What turn of phrase offers a new insight, new feeling, new possibility? Forget the cliches. And leave behind those anecdotes reprinted year after year in many of the preaching magazines, the *Cliff Notes* of sermon preparation. Preaching calls for the fresh sentence, the daring image, the delightful story. Sermons also need to be *deeply human*. The old homiletical idea of the preacher's not making personal references in the sermon is wrongheaded and should be ignored. The "I" of preaching is not narcissism, it is the "I" of invitation. Part of my calling is to express myself, my deepest humanity, in the sermon. When that happens, rather than blocking the Word of God, the Word becomes incarnate through my humanity. People who listen to sermons love humanity, are hungry for it. And well they should be, because when genuine humanity is expressed, it becomes divine. Ahh, the mystery of God. When all of it happens—the speaking and listening that happen in churches all over the world—it is magical. More than magical, it is inspiration that comes from God.

In this book, therefore, I offer sermons, but not just sermons. This book is designed for the individual reader or the Sunday school class, the personal seeker or the church study group. The format of this book is really quite simple. I started to realize through the years that many of my sermons fall within four different areas. *Anticipation* includes sermons that look forward to the coming activity of God in the world and in our lives. These are Advent and Lent-type sermons, sermons that call us to get ready, wake up, sit up, get moving, stop complaining, open our eyes. Why? Because the Lord is coming near. *Recognition* sermons are those sermons that ask us to see who God is, what God is doing, what is real and not real in life. Naming and recognizing the presence of God in our daily lives is crucial. The third section is *Celebration*. These sermons invite the listener to give thanks, enjoy, celebrate what is true and real in life. I'm afraid not enough sermons being preached in churches are celebration sermons. Mainline Protestants especially have been so heavy-handed with social awareness or so pitiful in the late-century demise of Protestantism that celebration has been in short supply. But if the kingdom of God is a party (this was the view of Jesus) then there's no way to have too much celebration. The last section is *Edification*. These sermons are offered simply to build up faith and understanding, to offer new insights about daily living.

These are sermons about relationships or families, life turning points, and moments of growth for the journey. In some ways, these categories are artificial, but they provide at least a general framework to think about our faith.

It continues to be amazing to me that people still respond to sermons. Preaching continues to change through the years, and it should change. But the fact that people such as the young couple I mentioned continue to be engaged by sermons is nothing short of remarkable. It is with a profound belief in the "remarkable" that these sermons are now passed on to a wider audience through this book. The reader should notice that in some ways the sermons have become essays. In other ways, I've tried to retain the oral quality of the sermon, attempting to write how I speak and how I hope I am heard.

Several years ago, *New Yorker* essayist E. B. White said, "Television has taken a big bite out of the written word. But words still count with me." And I gladly affirm the same of sermons. Internet. Television. Radio. Marketing. Advertising. VCRs. Walkmans. Communication happens incessantly. But is it really communication, that is to say, communion with something deep and important? To have a breakthrough moment, a moment when the preacher stands before his or her congregation, tells stories, offers part of his or her life, lays it out, and in that moment the listener is moved, strangely moved by some new idea or some important reaffirmation—for such a moment to happen is nothing less than marvelous.

I encourage readers, users really, of this book to read the scripture reading at the beginning of each chapter. Notice the section on biblical reflections. This section more than anything will give you some clues on how to use the Bible in a way that makes sense for today's world. Although I address this more completely in my book *Finding a Faith That Makes Sense,* these little comments will be helpful. Read the sermon text, and then if you are in a group situation, feel free to use the sermon feedback questions. One good way to begin the discussion is to ask the questions: *What in the sermon did you like? What touched you? What made a positive difference for you?*

To circle the divine is to move around and around the endless circle of God, our soul, the depth of human experience. Sometimes in that circling we are comforted. At other times we are challenged. But the circling, the learning, the growing, the experiencing don't cease. Within the sacred moment of preaching, listening, responding, we are indeed circling the great, great, great God of our journey.

SECTION I

Anticipation

1

Dazzled
by Glory

Scripture Text—Isaiah 40:1–11

Comfort, O comfort my people, says your God. Speak tenderly to Jerusalem, and cry to her that she has served her term, that her penalty is paid, that she has received from the LORD's hand double for all her sins. A voice cries out: "In the wilderness prepare the way of the LORD, make straight in the desert a highway for our God. Every valley shall be lifted up, and every mountain and hill be made low; the uneven ground shall become level, and the rough places a plain. Then the glory of the LORD shall be revealed, and all people shall see it together, for the mouth of the LORD has spoken." A voice says, "Cry out!" And I said, "What shall I cry?" All people are grass, their constancy is like the flower of the field. The grass withers, the flower fades, when the breath of the LORD blows upon it; surely the people are grass. The grass withers, the flower fades; but the word of our God will stand forever. Get you up to a high mountain, O Zion, herald of good tidings; lift up your voice with strength, O Jerusalem, herald of good tidings, lift it up, do not fear; say to the cities of Judah, "Here is your God!" See, the Lord GOD comes with might, and his arm rules for him; his reward is with him, and his recompense before him. He will feed his flock like a shepherd; he will gather the lambs in his arms, and carry them in his bosom, and gently lead the mother sheep.

Biblical Reflections

The book of Isaiah roughly falls into two parts. The first thirty-nine chapters portray the gloom and doom of God's judgment. Yet, with the opening of chapter 40, there is a new spirit, or at least another dimension of God's presence with the people of Israel, one of comfort and hope. In this chapter, the people are invited to make ready their lives for the end of the Babylonian exile and the coming of God in their lives. For this reason, this particular reading is often used during the Advent season as Christians ready themselves for the coming of God once again in the Christmas season. Additionally, this reading is used during Advent because it is linked to the story of John the Baptist, who prepared the way for Jesus.

What captured my imagination in preparing this sermon was the theme of comfort. What is comfort? How does the church provide comfort? How does each of us experience the comfort of God? Is comfort the mere soothing of feelings or is it more, perhaps even much more? I try to name some of the places in contemporary life where comfort is needed and where comfort is manifest. I don't have to tell you that it is much easier to name the places in the world devoid of comfort than it is to name the places where God's face is shining. But a sermon needs to do both, even as Christians need to see both the empty and full places in life.

Sermon Text

A few weeks ago, I had a chance to see one of the most disturbing and thought-provoking films I've seen in a long time. The movie was *Dead Man Walking.* Have you had a chance to see it?

It's the story of Sister Helen Prejean, a Catholic nun who finds herself ministering to a convicted criminal on death row. It's based on a true story. And given what is happening in our culture with more and more executions, it is a movie of burning relevance.

Frankly, I was skeptical about the film at first because I thought it might be one of those films either "for" or "against" the death penalty, and the truth is I don't care much for propaganda that tries to masquerade as art. But this film was different. Much to my surprise, I found myself deeply engaged with the movie.

It shows the anguish and pain of the victims and their families. And if you have ever been a victim of a crime, you know how vulnerable that makes you feel. But the movie also shows the human side of this criminal. It shows his mother. His brothers. His childhood. And caught in the middle is this Catholic nun, Sister Helen, and she is trying her best to bring God's comfort.

But there is one scene, one unforgettable scene, when the prison guard comes to get the criminal for his execution and calls down the hallway, "Dead man walking." Sister Helen is with him. The criminal's name is Matthew.

He desperately calls to her, "Don't leave me. Don't leave me now, Sister. Please, don't leave me."

She grabs his arm. Walks down the hall. They are both in tears. And walking to that execution, she then says one of the most remarkable lines I've ever heard. She says, "I want the last face you see on this earth to be a face of love."

The prophet Isaiah cries out the words, "Comfort, O comfort my people." And I don't know about you, but I love the sound of those words. "Comfort, O comfort my people." And maybe I love the words, maybe you love them too, because we know that there is so much of life that needs the comfort of God. In fact, there's not a person listening to this sermon that hasn't felt some need, some hope for comfort.

I've seen two unforgettable photographs recently in the *New York Times* that remind me of how desperate we are for God's comfort.

The first one was back in October. It was a picture of the AIDS Memorial Quilt that was unfurled at the base of the Washington Monument and stretched all the way to the Capitol building. Eleven blocks long. Thirty-seven thousand panels. Each panel a story of heartache and grief, personally decorated by family members with such items as baseball caps, patches from favorite denim jackets, little stuffed animals sewed to the squares. One reporter wrote, "For the most part, visitors to the quilt were as quiet as if they were at a shrine.... There were few sounds louder than sniffling, sobbing, and sighs."

The other photograph was also taken in Washington, D.C. It was taken on Veterans' Day in November at the Vietnam Memorial. I couldn't quite tell how old the man was; maybe he was in his late forties. He wore combat boots, a T-shirt, a pair of camouflage pants, and a jacket. And in the photograph you could see him standing next to that black wall with all those names, name after name after name, and his fingers were outstretched, touching the letters of the names as if he were reading braille.

"Comfort, O comfort my people, says your God." Of course, we need to hear of God's comfort. Of course, we need to feel God's comfort. We're as desperate for the comfort of God as was ancient Israel. This particular word of comfort is addressed to those who had lived in Babylonian exile, who had been in the desert of life, who had lived in the wilderness of captivity. And we've been there, too. Ask any Vietnam veteran; he'll tell you about wilderness. Ask any mother who has decorated a square of that quilt; she'll tell you about desert. And each of you, in your own way, from your own experience—you could talk about wilderness time, too.

But in this reading from Isaiah 40, we have a dramatic announcement of comfort. Isaiah tells the people that it's now time to stand up and dust yourself off. It's now time to start walking to the oasis in the desert. It's now time to let go of the past that's been demonizing your life. It's now time to quit making appearances on the *Ricki Lake Show*, telling everybody how bad the Babylonian exile was. It's now time to disband that little desert support group you've grown so fond of and begin really living your life. It's time!

And I'll tell you what else—it's time to see a face other than your own face of fear or your own face of bitterness that you see every morning in the mirror when you shave your face or comb your hair. It's time to stop looking at the faces of those people who have hurt you or abandoned you or mistreated you. It's time. It's time to see the face of God, and that is a face of love, of tenderness, a face of glory.

There are really two reasons why I like this reading from Isaiah.

First of all, this reading *acknowledges the reality of the desert.* Before there is comfort there has to be an acknowledgment of the desert. The desert might be AIDS. It might be war. It might be unemployment. It might be crime. It might be addiction. It might be the death of a loved one. It might be homesickness. One of the most important theological claims we make about God is that God acknowledges the desert experience of people.

But more than acknowledging it—I don't quite know how to express it this morning, except maybe to say that—God *lingers* with you in the desert. When you are in the desert, God says things like, "Take all the time you need. Be gentle with yourself. You don't have to be in a hurry." When you and I are in the desert, God says things like, "I'm not going anywhere. Let's just sit here together." And what's even more incredible is that God lingers with us in the desert even when we don't know that we're in the desert.

You see, I think if there could have been a special camera lens that could have picked up an infrared presence of God in Washington, D.C., we might have seen in that photograph God at that big quilt, saying to a mother, "Take all the time you need. I'll just, oh, I'll just mosey around until you're ready to go." Don't you think God would say something like that? Or don't you think that God might say to that veteran standing next to that memorial wall, "I'm not in any hurry. I'll just sit over here on the bench until it's time to go back home." Wouldn't God, the comforting God, say something like that?

What God knows, what many of us sometimes forget, is that you never bring comfort to other human beings until you're willing to linger with them in the desert. For God's sake, if you have a friend who's going through a hard time, whatever you do, don't give him or her advice. Don't say, "If I were you...." Don't preach a sermon. Don't try to tell them what they should be doing. Don't tell them to read a book, attend a lecture, take a course. God comforts you, and you comfort others, by learning how to linger with another. Too quickly we as Christians have wanted to "fix" the desert, but finally we have to acknowledge that the desert doesn't need fixing. The desert has its own mystery and meaning.

But you see, as much as I like the fact that God is with us in the desert, there's another part of this reading that I've come to love, namely, that part of God that *calls us to a mountaintop.* Listen to the inspiration of Isaiah (40:9):

> Get you up to a high mountain,
>   O Zion, herald of good tidings;
> lift up your voice with strength,
>   O Jerusalem, herald of good tidings,
>   lift it up, do not fear.

I love this language! I love it because it helps me see that although God is *with* me in the desert, it doesn't mean that God wants me to *stay* in the desert.

I think that's a concept important for us to hear this morning because what I see happening in our culture more and more is this pervasive sense of victimization. And what is victimization but staying in the desert way too long? The television talk shows not only perpetuate victimization, they also help to create it; just ask Jenny Jones, who recently staged a show with the repercussion of a senseless murder only days later. In spite of the fact that we have more people engaged in psychotherapy than ever before in the history of our nation, we don't seem to be getting any closer to wholeness. A recent survey indicated that more than 50 percent of our population is suffering in some form or another from depression. What that means is that depression has now become the statistical norm. We've had a proliferation of support-type groups, every one of them important to be sure, but at what point is the group nudging us toward the mountain of wholeness, or holding us back in the desert of brokenness?

Please don't misunderstand what I'm saying today. There are real victims. There are real hurts and wounds that cast us into the wilderness. Some have had childhood wounds and conflicts that are beyond the human imagination. And for the church to be the church, we need to be a place where divine comfort is brought to people. But God's comfort also prods and pushes us to the mountaintop of well-being. After all, the word *comfort* literally means "a bringing together of strength." And that assumes that God has strength. And that assumes that every one of you has a certain reservoir of strength, too. Comfort is more than empathy; it's the renewal of strength.

No, you can't skip the desert. Sometimes the dark night of the soul must be endured. The hard work of recovery must be engaged. Sometimes the painstaking work of therapy is the work of God. But it's the mountaintop, this gift of wholeness and well-being—for me, for you, for all the children in God's world—that God calls us to receive as a gift and to take on as our mission.

Perhaps it should be said, however, that it's seldom the case that we live in the desert and then wake up one morning suddenly dazzled by the glory of God on top of the mountain. There might be instant mountains out there, but probably not many of them. Typically, we find a little desert, then we find a little mountain. We drift back to the desert but then make our way back to the mountain. But do you see that it's one thing to move back and forth between mountain and desert, and it's completely another to forget that the mountain of God is there? I think one of the most profoundly hopeful things we can do as Christians is to believe that wholeness for our lives and the lives of others is possible. Not perfection. A perfectionistic drive becomes a desert in and of itself. Perfection is not what I'm talking about. The key is wholeness.

Isaiah envisions a new coming of the presence of God. Land is cleared. A new superhighway is built. The rough places are made smooth. And yes, desert is replaced by mountain. And this divine one who comes, comes with a face not of punishment, not of anger, not of indifference—but this one who comes has a face of tenderness and love. It's a face of comfort.

How many times during the holidays have we poked our head inside that manger of Bethlehem needing to see that face, wanting to see that face for just a moment, that face we know will never turn away from us? And seeing that face is there some feeling, some impulse that makes you want to follow? Is there some strange comfort you feel by seeing this face, this face of light, this face of love? And could this face, this one unforgettable face, could it touch you, move you, could it make you a better person? Could it move you to put your arms around that mother who gently weeps over one particular panel of that AIDS Memorial Quilt? Could the face inside that manger, that face of dazzling light, could it move you to stand beside that veteran reading the wall?

This face, this face of God, this face of Christmas, could it come to you this year? Could it linger with you in not just any desert but your desert? Could you see this face of love and imagine that you've spent enough time in the desert? Time to move. Time to grow. Time to change. Could this face of comfort give you enough strength so as to start climbing the mountain of your life again?

Questions for Reflection

1. Where are the places in our society that need the most comfort?

2. Where have you seen the "face of God" in your daily life lately?

3. How can the church become more of a source of comfort, surrounding others with strength and thus continuing the comforting presence of God in the world?

2

Will the Real Christmas Please Stand Up?

Scripture Text—John 1:6–8, 19–28

There was a man sent from God, whose name was John. He came as a witness to testify to the light, so that all might believe through him. He himself was not the light, but he came to testify to the light....This is the testimony given by John when the Jews sent priests and Levites from Jerusalem to ask him, "Who are you?" He confessed and did not deny it, but confessed, "I am not the Messiah." And they asked him, "What then? Are you Elijah?" He said, "I am not." "Are you the prophet?" He answered, "No." Then they said to him, "Who are you? Let us have an answer for those who sent us. What do you say about yourself?" He said, "I am the voice of one crying out in the wilderness, 'Make straight the way of the Lord,' as the prophet Isaiah said." Now they had been sent from the Pharisees. They asked him, "Why then are you baptizing if you are neither the Messiah, nor Elijah, nor the prophet?" John answered them, "I baptize with water. Among you stands one whom you do not know, the one who is coming after me; I am not worthy to untie the thong of his sandal." This took place in Bethany across the Jordan where John was baptizing.

Biblical Reflections

Although this is an Advent and Christmas season reading for the church, it's obviously not the traditional Christmas story as told in Matthew and Luke. Yet, John's reading is appropriate at Christmas because it moves us to a more philosophical understanding of Jesus' appearance in the world and, as this reading indicates, helps us understand the preparatory role of John the Baptist in the unfolding story of Jesus.

Evidently there was recognition that John was a dynamic and powerful religious leader, but the question of his exact identity remained for his contemporaries, as for us, something of an enigma. John's role as prophet was to speak forth the word of God. That is the meaning of the word prophesy. Predicting the future had little if any role in biblical prophecy. To be a prophet meant to preach a word of God for a contemporary situation. In the tradition of Judaism, prophets often helped the religious community to clarify its values and, thus, shape its identity. Certainly John plays out this role. Additionally, the prophets pointed their fingers toward events in the world that indicated God was really at work in the lives of people. Indeed, John does this as well as pointing his finger toward Jesus.

In this sermon I ask listeners to pause in the mad rush of Christmas and clarify their values. What is Christmas all about? What do we really want for Christmas? What do we hope to be when the tinsel has been taken down and the tree left out on the side of the road for the sanitation department? Holiday seasons can be wonderful, but only if we allow them to call us home to something deeper and not drive us further away from the deepest longings we already possess. I continue to be surprised at the number of people who either miss the holidays or who avoid them in one way or another. Christmas can be an incredible time of renewal, but only if we awaken to its true essence.

Sermon Text

It's getting closer. Much closer. Only ten more days until Christmas, and as it gets closer the pressure is rising, the stress is increasing, the obligations are building. I noticed in the newspaper this week that even the cartoon character Cathy was feeling the pressure when she said, "I'm trying to smash a size 16 schedule into a size 2 time slot." And I know that some of you are trying to do the same.

Many of us today are here in this sanctuary, and we remember Christmas. We want Christmas. We need Christmas. We would even like to replicate Christmas. And even though we know better, we tend to fall year after year for this idealization that has become such a part of Christmas.

Hanging above my desk at home is a print by Norman Rockwell titled *Christmas at Stockbridge*. There's snow on the street, children riding their sleds, and the famous Red Lion Inn glowing with Christmas lights. I look at that ideal picture of Christmas, and I must admit, even though I know it's impossible to reproduce such a Christmas, something inside me feels nostalgic for that kind of Christmas. I would love to go to Stockbridge for Christmas!

Do you ever feel that kind of Christmas nostalgia?

Let's face it. We want old carols to wrap themselves around us like old quilts. We want a house that looks like a house in *Southern Living* magazine. We want a tree that looks like a tree found in *Good Housekeeping*. We want our daughters to look like they stepped out of a Laura Ashley catalog. We want the family dog sitting on a tartan plaid cushion in front of the fireplace just like they do in the L. L. Bean catalog. We want our sons to look like a page out of the Lands' End catalog. Let's be honest. We want "chestnuts roasting on an open fire." We want a glimpse of a "wonderful life." And though the chances are remote, very remote here in Texas, wouldn't you like to have just a touch of a "white Christmas"?

The problem with this scripture reading from the Gospel of John is that it's not so much about the baby Jesus as it is about the man who prepared the way for Jesus, namely John the Baptist. And John the Baptist was and is a problem.

You never knew how he would show up at the Sunday school Christmas party. The ladies in their nice dresses. The men in their suits with those crazy holiday ties. But John, John might march through the front door wearing something like a burlap sack for a shirt, his hair dusty and tangled from the wind. He was a desert man, you know, his skin dry and leathery from the sun. And while others brought desserts and casseroles, John often would bring a jar of honey and a bag of locusts as his contribution to the holiday meal. Obviously he had never seen an episode of *Martha Stewart Living*. John was edgy, dangerous, challenging.

Yet, somehow we need John the Baptist today. We need him because he is—not was, but is—a voice crying out in the wilderness. And the reason why his voice is so important is because it is a voice that calls us to be clear about what is real and what is not real in life, about what is full and what is empty in life, about what is important and what is not important in life. And I'll tell you what else, we need John the Baptist to help us see what is Christmas and what is not Christmas.

You see, John's whole mission in life might be understood as *reality clarification*. There were those, you see, who were so drawn to John, to his rugged preaching and no-nonsense theology, that they started to believe that John himself was the Messiah. You can almost hear them. "You're the one. You're the one, John. We'll follow you. You're the Messiah." Even dignitaries from the city would take a tour bus out to the desert to hear him preach and, after the sermon reached its crescendo, would ask, "Who exactly are you? Where did you go to school? Are you the one who is to come?"

I wonder if there was a little part of John—not a big part, but that small opportunistic part of him—that wanted to seize the moment and say, "Yes. Why, yes. Of course, yes. I am the Messiah." But he didn't. John knew, not only *what* was most important in life, but also *who* was most important in life. A lesson all of us struggle to learn. Think about it this morning. What is it that defines your life today? What ultimate values are you living with this morning? What is it that is most important to you?

John points his finger toward Jesus. "I'm not the Messiah. I am not the light of God. He is the one. He is the Messiah. I baptize, yes, but there's one coming after me who is much greater than I. He's the light of God."

Could it be that one reason we need John the Baptist during this season of Advent is that we, too, are faced, not so much with false Christs, but with false Christmases? We make all kinds of choices during the Christmas season, how we spend our time, how we spend our money, where we will go for the holidays. But the most essential question finally becomes— What Christ and what kind of Christmas will we find this year?

How many of us *overidealize* Christmas? We long so much for the promise of Christmas that we expect too much, become unrealistic, find ourselves working to recreate some ideal picture in our brain that can never be recreated.

How many of us *overcommit* at Christmas? We think we can fit one more event into our social schedule, host one more party at the house, provide refreshments at one more function at school.

How many of us *overspend* at Christmas? We don't want to disappoint the kids. We want the house to look at least as nice as the neighbors'. We don't want to appear cheap at the gift exchange.

How many of us *overindulge* at Christmas? The holiday hangover becomes acceptable. The overeating makes us feel awful. Even the excessiveness of advertising and shopping somehow drain life from us.

How many of us *overachieve* at Christmas? Here's the big chance to be super-mom, super-dad, super-grandparent, but somehow it feels a little bit like it's out of control, out of balance, and instead of seeing a Christmas star you feel more like a burned-out meteorite.

How many of us *overexpect* at Christmas? We want love, understanding, thoughtfulness, not to mention sensitivity, creativity, and that perfect present from that person we love the most. And often we spend our holidays being disappointed in another human being, usually someone in our family.

What I like about John the Baptist, if indeed you can think of him as likeable, is that he becomes a reality check for me. He reminds me that the point of Christmas is to see Christ, to see this great light of God that has come into the world through the birth of Jesus. And although I may have all kinds of expectations around Christmas, if I miss this light, this message, this experience, then I have missed it all. The whole point of holiday seasons is to call us home, not to some literal house, but to the religious home within ourselves where faith and feeling are more real, more vital, more dynamic.

No matter how many times I hear it I never tire of O. Henry's *The Gift of the Magi*. You know the story. Jim and Della are deeply in love and shockingly poor. It is Christmas time, and they want to buy each other the most beautiful, most expensive presents. Yet, it's simply not possible.

Jim makes the decision that he can buy Della a Christmas gift, but only if he will sell his most prized possession, a gold pocket watch, an heirloom handed down to him from his father. Selflessly, he sells the watch, goes to the store, and buys Della a set of beautiful tortoiseshell combs that will hold in place her long, lovely hair.

Meanwhile, Della wants to buy Jim a Christmas present, but she has no money either. Therefore, she cuts off all her gorgeous hair, sells the hair to a wig maker, and then takes the money and buys Jim a Christmas present—a gold chain for his pocket watch.

On Christmas morning when they open their packages, they each find a gift they can no longer use, but what they have found is the wonderful, mysterious, awe-inspiring gift of Christmas. And it is such a gift because they have given themselves.

In our high-tech and harried world, that story seems so quaint, so harmless, antique-like really, but I think each of us secretly longs for a Christmas half as meaningful as that Christmas. It's the real joy, the real meaning, the real essence of Christmas—that's what the heart wants. It's not found in the perfectionism expected of either ourselves or others. It's not found in the idealism displayed in a mail-order catalog. It's not found in the materialism that has become the false Christ of our age. Christmas is discovered when, in the words of John's Gospel, we find a way to "behold his glory," glory in the form of one who loves us, who forgives us, who calls us home to himself.

In his book *Returning,* Dan Wakefield begins his spiritual autobiography like this:

"One balmy spring morning in Hollywood, a month or so before my forty-eighth birthday, I woke up screaming. I got out of bed, went into the next room, sat down on a couch, and screamed again....It was a response to the reality that another morning had broken in a life I could only deal with sedated by wine, loud noise, moving images, and wired to electronic games....The day I woke up screaming I grabbed from among my books an old Bible I hadn't opened for nearly a quarter of a century. With a desperate instinct I turned to the Twenty-third Psalm and read it over, several times...."

A few months later, Dan Wakefield would venture out alone, walk down a street as a solitary figure, and go to a Christmas Eve church service. He hadn't been to church since he was a child. He writes of that Christmas and that church in these words: "I looked inside and saw a beginning."

I cannot help but wonder if, even as Christmas is coming closer, there might be some new spiritual beginning trying to come closer to you and to me, too. Do you know that's the meaning of religion? Religion literally means *to bind back together.* To take our lives and bind them back to God, to take our emptiness so that it might be filled by God, to take our brokenness so that it might be healed by God. That's religion.

Simone Weil once wrote that "God and human beings are like two lovers who have, due to some terrible mix-up, missed each other."

If it's true that you and I have almost missed God, then the heart of the Christmas story is about the lover God trying desperately to find us. God finding a burned-out writer like Dan Wakefield. God finding us the way Jim found Della and Della found Jim on Christmas morning. This God doesn't demand some kind of holiday perfection from us. And this God doesn't demand that we overachieve to prove our worth. And this God doesn't expect our lives or the lives of our families to be picture perfect for the December issue of *Good Housekeeping.* And aren't you glad that our lives don't have to look like a holiday catalog either?

This desperate lover, God, comes home to us in order to bring us home to ourselves. That's the work of the real Christ. And that's the real magic of Christmas. Get ready. It's coming closer. Don't miss it. It's almost here. It's almost Christmas.

Questions for Reflection

1. Do you feel nostalgic at Christmas? What is it that you miss most? Is there a way to reclaim part of your past and let go of other parts?

2. Have you ever been caught up in the idealism of Christmas or any other holiday season? What is it that snags you the most, and then drives you and others crazy? (Be honest here.)

3. What is one positive step for your faith you would like to take at this point in your life?

3

Watching the
Cherry Trees Blossom

Scripture Text—Mark 13:32–37

But about that day or hour no one knows, neither the angels in heaven, nor the Son, but only the Father. Beware, keep alert; for you do not know when the time will come. It is like a man going on a journey, when he leaves home and puts his slaves in charge, each with his work, and commands the doorkeeper to be on the watch. Therefore, keep awake—for you do not know when the master of the house will come, in the evening, or at midnight, or at cockcrow, or at dawn, or else he may find you asleep when he comes suddenly. And what I say to you I say to all: Keep awake.

Biblical Reflections

This reading from the Gospel of Mark is one of the more challenging and potentially troubling readings upon which to base a sermon. Typically this reading is used on the first Sunday of Advent, a season in which the church anticipates the birth of Jesus. Yet, this reading isn't about the birth of Jesus at all. Instead, it is about what is sometimes called the "second coming" of Christ, an expression, by the way, that isn't used in the Bible but which refers to the idea that Christ will return to earth and establish in some form God's rule over all people. It is always confusing to people as they listen to this reading during the Advent and Christmas season.

What is helpful to know is that this scripture text comes from a particular type of literature and thinking called "apocalyptic." Apocalyptic literature typically employs strong, vivid symbols in communicating the activity of God in the world. The most famous apocalyptic literature is the book of Revelation. In Revelation, one sees wild and grotesque symbols, vivid imagery, powerful contrasts between what is good and bad, God and evil, heaven and earth. Apocalyptic literature also portrays the coming of God into the world, replacing the present worldly powers with the spiritual powers of Christ.

What I try to do in the sermon is help people see that the "coming of God" is not something that happened once, or even twice. God's coming is forever present in the eternal now of God's very being. God comes or at least tries to come to our lives again and again and again. Our job as Christians is to open our eyes and find the activity of God in daily life. To miss it is to miss God, not because God didn't show up, but because we were too limited to really see. For this reason, this reading becomes especially appropriate for the season of Advent. True, Christ was born two thousand years ago. But it's also true that Christ, God's very expression of creative and transforming love, is wanting to be born in our world again and again. Therefore, as the scripture suggests, our job is to watch!

Sermon Text

If you had been in Japan this past April, you would have noticed that the parks and public gardens were filled with people. Thousands of people. You would have seen small tents dotting the landscape, along with portable tables replete with flowers, food, and wine. It's a national party called *hanami*, which literally means *viewing the flowers*. You would have seen adults dressed in suits and beautiful dresses, children playing in the grass with their friends, and adults furiously clicking their cameras.

And the flowers they came to see are the delicate blossoms found only on the cherry trees. The Japanese are passionate about cherry blossoms. They have cherry-blossom rice cakes, cherry-blossom ice cream, cherry-blossom tea. In fact, when a high school senior used to apply for college, he would receive a letter from the university simply reading: *The Cherry Blossoms Are Blooming—**Acceptance.*** Or *The Cherry Blossoms Are Lost—**Rejection.***

But it's this concept—the concept of waiting and watching, taking time to celebrate something as subtle and delicate and beautiful as a cherry blossom—that I think is so intriguing.

It is this theme of watching and waiting that we find this morning in our reading from Mark's Gospel. Remember now, Mark was writing to a church struggling with the specific experience of waiting for God. They had confessed their faith in Jesus Christ. They had reenacted the gospel story through Christian baptism. And now they are waiting. Waiting for Christ to return. Waiting for the kingdom of God to be established on earth. Waiting to take their place on one of the glorious committees of God's new age.

But their waiting started to last longer and longer, it was pulled and stretched like saltwater taffy, and slowly their waiting started to feel endless. And don't forget that while they were waiting, the Roman emperor Nero turned up the temperature of governmental persecution. There had been a massive fire in the capital city, Rome, and, like all good politicians, Nero needed someone to blame. And so he blamed the Christians. "Those Christians, those strange people called Christians, they're the ones who started the fire. They're the ones who are a threat to our city!" And so he persecuted them with slander, with physical abuse, with horrific death.

This is why Mark reminds the church of the words of Jesus: "You don't know what day or hour the Son will return. Only God knows that. Your job is to stay awake. Be alert. Your job is to keep watching and waiting because you never know when that time will come." And to make the point crystal clear, Jesus tells a little story. "It's like when the boss goes on a business trip and you're left in charge of the company. Don't think you can fool around, get lazy, skip out, and play golf every afternoon. You never know when the boss will catch an early flight home and come back to work. Listen, here's how you wait," says Jesus. "Keep your eyes open, and stay awake!"

The truth is that it's hard, isn't it, to stay awake to God? Hard to keep our eyes open to our own souls, to what we know is most important in life. After all, isn't there something deep within your soul that you're waiting for or that's waiting for you? Isn't there something of spiritual significance that has been calling for you, but you can't quite, can't quite seem to stay awake for it? Isn't there some change in your family that you can't quite wait on?

Let's be careful here this morning. For Jesus, waiting isn't some La-Z-Boy passivity. Waiting means we are awake to the spiritual presence of God. It means we are engaged in the spiritual mission of God. It means we celebrate the spiritual comings of God. That's waiting. And although I know there are some Christians who seem to be consumed with what they call the "second coming" of Christ, reading the signs, figuring out the symbols in the book of Revelation, nevertheless, I would encourage you to become consumed with what we might call the "daily comings" of Christ. The resonating questions on this first Sunday of Advent become something like: How is Christ discovered in daily life? Where is Christ found in daily life? When is Christ born in daily life? And even,

How do I become Christ for others in daily life? These, you see, are the questions for our lives of waiting.

I learned a little bit about waiting when I moved to Texas in September and had to go to the license branch. Have you ever had to wait at the license branch? It's a real education! Granted, I had something of an unusual situation when I arrived because on the trip down here my wallet was stolen. I had never lost a wallet in my entire life. All my cash. All my credit cards. Gone. My Social Security card. Gone. And, of course, my driver's license was gone, too.

Well, I knew I had to get a Texas driver's license sooner or later, and so I went out to the license branch to take care of this little detail of life. I explained to this woman, who by the way I'm sure at one time or another had been a prison guard somewhere, that I had a driver's license, that it was from Kentucky, but that I didn't really have a license because it had been stolen, but now here I was, the new minister of University Christian Church, and I was ready to get a Texas driver's license. I was even smiling at the beginning of this process!

I've done enough public speaking to detect that two things were happening as I was telling her this story. First of all, I could tell that this woman had heard it all before. Second, she had never taken a pastoral counseling class because she could care less about the tale of my missing wallet!

She sent me on my way, and, believe me, every step required waiting. Did you know you have to get your license plates before you can get your driver's license? I stood in line to do that. But did you know you have to have an inspection on your car before you can get your plates? I stood in line for the inspection. Did you know that you have to prove that your car is insured before you can get a license plate, inspection, and driver's license? I stood in line to get insurance. Guess what? After I got insurance, I had the privilege of going back and standing in line for the inspection, the plates, and the license again. And did you know that if you don't have a valid driver's license you must take the written exam? I stood in line for an hour and a half with a bunch of fifteen-year-olds in order to take the written test. I thought I was going to break out in acne again! And did you know that if you don't have a valid driver's license, after you take the written test, you have to take the driving test? And did you know that to get on the schedule for the driving test you have to arrive at the license branch at 6:30 in the morning, even though they don't open until 8:00 in the morning, otherwise they have too many people and you don't get to take your test? I waited. I waited in line. I saw the sunrise at the license branch that morning!

Finally, it was my turn to take the driving test. I pulled my car around, and another less-than-pleasant lady was ready to give me a driving test. She looked at my car and said, "Where are your plates?"

I said, "Oh, I just got them yesterday. They're in the trunk. I didn't know you needed them on the car. I still have my Kentucky plates on, but look, I'll show them to you."

She said, "I can't give you a test without Texas plates."

I said, "Oh, come on. I have the plates. They're right here." I pulled them out of the trunk.

By this point I'm desperate. I'm a man on the edge. I realize that my driving destiny, no, my whole identity as a citizen of this country is in the hands of this grumpy woman. But while I'm talking, I notice she's writing something on her pad of paper. She pulls it off and hands it to me.

I said, "What's this?"

She said, "It's a citation for driving a car without proper plates."

She gave me a ticket! It was only a warning, but still, it was a ticket! This woman gave me a ticket!

I pull my car out of line. Go and get my plates on. Come back. Wait in line some more, and finally take the driving test.

I passed. Aren't you proud of me?

I go back into the license branch, stand in line to have my picture taken (by the way, no kidding, the computers were down). Finally, I stood in front of that camera. Then do you know what the woman who took my picture said to me? She had the nerve to say to me, "Now smile."

Waiting. Waiting. Waiting. My hunch is that every one of us here this morning is waiting for something. And our waiting is hard because while we wait we sometimes think it will never end, think we'll never get well, think the project will never be completed, think life will never be good again, think we'll never recover from this grief. Waiting is hard because we feel helpless in our waiting, feel all alone in our waiting, feel that we don't know what to do in our waiting. And let's face it, waiting is hard because we get tired of waiting. Waiting is tough business.

Jesus knew that sometimes faith in God is expressed in waiting and watching for God. But his definition of waiting is more like getting ready, like making preparations, like celebrating those moments when God's presence is made known to us. I think the waiting of Jesus is more like the Japanese day of *hanami*, waiting for God to bloom like the blossoms of a cherry tree.

Do you know what I think would make for a great Advent project? I think it would be exciting to see how many moments you could claim during this month of December as moments of God's blossoming. Waiting isn't easy, I know, nor is the stress and emotion of the holidays, but how many experiences might you have this month that could bring you closer to God? It's not flashy, I know, but could it be that our goal for the season of Advent is simply to pay attention to the many ways God comes to us?

And we can turn it around and say that not only do we look for the coming of God during this holiday season, but we also seek to become a little bit of God for others. How many ways could we share the spirit of Christ during Advent? How many ways could we become the coming of God for another person? How many times during the month of December could we become the birth of Christ for another?

You see, the truth is, it's rather misleading to talk about the first coming of Christ or the second coming of Christ because Christ is always coming to us. And it's also true that every time we move toward another person with love, with mercy, with compassion, Christ is brought to our world again.

Of all the times I waited at the license branch, there was one person who provided me with something of a human conversation. He and I stood outside the door at 6:30 one morning. He was wearing a pair of jeans, a denim jacket, dusty work boots. He was Hispanic. He had just moved here from New Mexico. He told me about New Mexico, how he loved New Mexico, how he had moved here because of work. I was reading the morning paper, and as I finished a section of the *Star-Telegram*, I would pass it on to him. We read the paper together that morning. I don't even know his name. He doesn't know mine. But while we waited, for a few hours at least, two strangers became friends.

And when that happens, I know, at least for that moment, that I'm in the territory of God's coming, because it's subtle and beautiful and meaningful—like the blossoming of a cherry tree. Or like the cry of a baby from a manger.

Questions for Reflection

1. Can you name a quiet, subtle, meaningful moment in your life when you felt the presence of God coming near to you?

2. If watching means assertive activity in the name of God, what is it that you would like to begin doing to make your Christian life more active and engaged?

3. How might you or your church become more the presence of God for others during a busy holiday season like Christmas?

4

Don't
Miss It!

Scripture Text—Matthew 25:1–13

Then the kingdom of heaven will be like this. Ten bridesmaids took their lamps and went to meet the bridegroom. Five of them were foolish, and five were wise. When the foolish took their lamps, they took no oil with them; but the wise took flasks of oil with their lamps. As the bridegroom was delayed, all of them became drowsy and slept. But at midnight there was a shout, "Look! Here is the bridegroom! Come out to meet him." Then all those bridesmaids got up and trimmed their lamps. The foolish said to the wise, "Give us some of your oil, for our lamps are going out." But the wise replied, "No! There will not be enough for you and for us; you had better go to the dealers and buy some for yourselves." And while they went to buy it, the bridegroom came, and those who were ready went with him into the wedding banquet; and the door was shut. Later the other bridesmaids came also, saying, "Lord, lord, open to us." But he replied, "Truly I tell you, I do not know you." Keep awake therefore, for you know neither the day nor the hour.

Biblical Reflections

This particular parable is actually part of a trio of parables found in Matthew 25 that deal with a real-life problem in the life of the early church, namely, the delay of the *parousia*, the coming of Christ. This was no doubt one of the most disturbing issues in the early church. Fully confident that Jesus would return and begin some earthly manifestation of the kingdom of God, the early Christians had to readjust their expectations, learning how to live with an "absent Jesus." It would be hard to overstate what a major disappointment and challenge this presented to the early Christians. The message of the parable, as it is presented to us by Matthew, is clearly one of preparation, readiness, and daily faithfulness.

Reading the parables of Jesus invites the playful use of our imaginations. Too often we get caught up in trying to figure out the parable or distilling the single message of the parable. No doubt, parables have a message quality to them. But more than mere message, parables invite readers to enter into the world of the story. Living in that world, we not only listen for the message, but we also listen to our feelings, our hunches, and inklings. We experience insights while reading the parable. In this particular parable, we are invited to imagine how often we miss God's coming—not so much a "second coming" of Jesus, but the many times God's activity is present in our world and lives, and due to a variety of reasons, we simply miss it.

When reading a parable, or for that matter any scripture, it is important to ask, "What in the story really captures my imagination?" Whatever the answer becomes is often the very word God is trying to speak to our lives. Thus, reading the parable becomes a sacred act of listening to our souls—an adventure really, of discovering God, ourselves, our neighbor. In this sermon, I recall one experience in my life that reminded me of the presence of God, and I invite you to enter into the practice of listening to your life, as well.

Sermon Text

I want to begin this morning by sharing with you an experience I had in California this past summer. It probably won't take you too long to figure out that I love California. I love the climate, the ocean, the mountains, and I even like the people. Now they're a little different, to be sure, but I like them. And fortunately I've been able to dodge all the major earthquakes.

One morning this summer my friend Dale Martlage and I decided to go out for breakfast. I rarely eat breakfast. But when I'm on vacation, I love to go out for breakfast. Lots of coffee. Read the newspaper. Just relax. And did you know that those omelets have no fat grams when you're on vacation? Well, we went out for breakfast that morning, and we had one of those conversations that jumped and moved from topic to topic. It was great fun!

After breakfast we were driving back to the house, in a convertible of course, and I saw this sign that read, VILLA MONTALVO. I asked Dale,

"What's Villa Montalvo?" He said, "Pull in, and I'll show you." I pulled into the entrance, drove up a long winding drive, past beautiful gardens and enormous eucalyptus trees, and then I saw this beautiful mansion. It was gorgeous.

I learned that Villa Montalvo had been built years ago as something of a summer residence for the governor of California, that the governor would bring guests there and host these picturesque parties out on the front lawn with live music and people going in and out of the mansion. Today the residence has been turned into a small performing arts center. Behind the mansion is an amphitheater for concerts.

It was about ten o'clock on a Friday morning when we were there. We walked around some of the gardens, noticed the architecture of the house, and then as we came around the back of the mansion we noticed there was a single grand piano sitting on the stage. A young Asian man was there tuning the piano. A second or two later there was another man who came around the corner of the stage.

I looked at Dale and whispered, "Do you know who that is?"

He said, "No, who is it?"

I said, "That's Andre Watts. That's the great concert pianist Andre Watts." I couldn't believe it. I had seen him on PBS so many times, had heard his music, seen his picture on the front of CD covers. Evidently he was going to perform there that night, but now there he was all alone at that grand piano.

We quietly walked up the steps of the amphitheatre, sat down, and waited. Andre Watts sort of looked at us like we were two pigeons in front of a park bench. But then he turned away, looked down at the keys, and started to play. The music that came from that piano was astonishing. He played and played. He played for one solid hour. And I'll never forget his hands. They moved with such incredible grace upon the black and white keys.

And from time to time I would look at Dale or he would look over at me, and we would just shake our heads and practically giggle over the delight of being in the presence of this music. It was awesome! That's what it was. It was an awesome surprise, totally unexpected, a completely undeserved moment of grace. And the best part about it, it was free!

I want you to think about surprise this morning because I think that's what is at the heart of this parable from the Gospel of Matthew—the element of surprise. The presence of God—or if you like Matthew's concept, the kingdom of God—is like a surprise. And yes, there is a warning in the parable not to fall asleep, but it's not a warning like the message printed on the side of a pack of cigarettes. It's really an encouragement, a warning that is more like an invitation from God that we find in this parable. And the invitation is to live life with faith and openness and expectation for the surprising presence of God. The parable reminds us: Don't miss it. Don't be caught off guard. Get ready to receive it. God's grace comes to us, not in the certainty of calculation, but in the serendipity of surprise.

Granted, the parable itself may seem a little strange to us. There's this wedding. The bridesmaids are all standing around in those funny, puffy pink dresses that bridesmaids seem to wear. Remember now, this was in the days before electricity, and so they are standing in one of the old Sunday school rooms holding their oil lamps, waiting and waiting and waiting for the groom to make his appearance and the ceremony to begin. And as they wait, the wicks get shorter and shorter, and the oil supplies get lower and lower.

I have no idea what's happened to the groom. Maybe he's stuck in traffic. I don't know. Maybe he has cold feet. Who knows? I would like to think that maybe he's making a quick stop at the bank because he forgot the minister's honorarium. I don't really know why he's late. But the point of the parable really is not to speculate on why he's delayed; the parable invites us to learn how to live a life of faith even in the midst of those times when it seems that God is delayed.

You see, for the early Christians this was an especially poignant parable. When they were baptized, they fully believed that Jesus was going to return very quickly and establish in some form or another the kingdom of God. They wanted the kingdom of God, to be sure, but they never had bargained for this long line of waiting to get into it. In fact, one of the biggest faith questions they had to face was, How do we believe in God even while we wait for God?

Some of you know what waiting is like, don't you? Right now I can see a daughter waiting at a hospital by the side of her mother. She has been waiting so long, and she knows that when she gets up in the morning there will still be more waiting. I see a man waiting in his living room for a phone call about a job, about a job he desperately needs. He's waiting. I see a young man sitting in a doctor's office waiting, waiting for the results of an AIDS test. Waiting. Waiting. I see a college senior waiting to find out what school she will enter next year. Waiting.

This parable does not eliminate the waiting in life. But what it does suggest is that even in the waiting there is a surprising presence of God that we should look for, long for, hope for. And to be a Christian means that we've got to be ready. We've got to keep enough oil in our lamps. We've got to keep our eyes open, because we never know when God will surprise us.

My friend Brother David Steindl-Rast has written, "To recognize that everything is surprising is the first step toward recognizing that everything is a gift." And it's true. Because what I can tell you out of my own experience is that when I am living with a sense of delight and surprise, I am grateful, and when I am grateful, I am most alive. And the times when I feel the deadness of my life, when I find myself in moods of resignation and defeat, it is because I have closed my eyes to the surprises of God's grace.

I think of that little verse in the book of Ephesians that reads: "Sleeper, awake! Rise from the dead, and Christ will shine on you." And what I love about that little verse is that it was originally recited by the congregation during a person's baptism. It was recited because the essence of being a baptized Christian is being an awake human being! *Sleeper, awake! Rise from the dead, and Christ will shine on you.* It almost sounds like a chant, doesn't it? *Sleeper, awake! Rise from the dead, and Christ will shine on you.* Maybe when we have baptisms we should have cheerleaders leading us in this little chant. *Sleeper, awake! Rise from the dead, and Christ will shine on you.* I'm not going to sing it. I sang in a sermon two weeks ago, and not one choir member invited me to join their "exclusive" little club. But you get the idea. To be a Christian means to be awake to the surprises of God.

I recently read a humorous story about a rabbi who lived in a small Russian village. The rabbi had experienced some strong dreams telling him that the Messiah was going to visit this remote little village, but the rabbi was fearful that the Messiah might not be able to find the village. Therefore, the people of the village helped the rabbi construct a tall lookout tower on the main road. And then, of course, they hired someone to sit up in the tower and look for the Messiah. One day, a friend stopped by and yelled up at the watchman, "How do you like the new job?" The watchman yelled back, "The pay's not much, but it's steady work."

Do you see that part of our steady work as Christians is looking and searching and getting ready for the surprises of God? Do you see that part of spirituality is learning how to be ready for those surprises, learning how to recognize those surprises, learning how to name those surprises of God in the world?

And believe me, finding the surprises of God in the midst of the waiting is not easy. I mean, it's easy to name those events in our world that seem devoid of God. All you have to do is listen to the news for one night and you'll hear stories of refugees in Zaire or the violent murder of a child in Fort Worth or the devastation of a cyclone in India or the racism that still exists even in the most respectable companies, like Texaco. It's easy to name those moments in life that seem so far from the goodness of God.

As Christians, we cannot ignore the suffering in God's world. Whether it's our own or the suffering of our neighbor, we can't ignore it. But one way, it's not the only way, but one way we respond to the suffering of the world is by having the faith and imagination to name those places in life where the goodness of God is seen and felt and exhibited. And these surprising places of God won't take away the world's suffering, but they will at least become reminders that there is grace in this world.

You cannot believe the number of times I've thought about that day at Villa Montalvo and the impromptu concert I experienced with Andre Watts. It was such a surprise. That day for me has become, not just a memory, but a metaphor. If we will ask our curious questions of life, if we will get off the beaten path of life, if we will live life with a little more wonder, open our eyes a little wider, let our hearts feel a little more, then the surprises of God might just happen. It makes me think that maybe we don't necessarily need to wait for a miracle of God to drop out of the sky and hit us on the head. Maybe the miracles of God are happening all the time, maybe they're swarming around our heads like summer mosquitoes every day, and all we need to do is see them.

I read a story a few years ago in the *Christian Science Monitor* by a woman who was reflecting on her childhood piano teacher, Mrs. Baker. The woman wrote that her strongest memory was that during her piano lesson Mrs. Baker, heavy with perfume and makeup, would get right up into her face, purse her lips, and say, "Play *deep* dear, play *deep* into the keys. That's how you must always play. *Deep* into the keys."

It's true. That is how we need to play. And live. And die. Deep into the keys. That's what this parable is about. It's about being deep into the keys. And I know you can live that way. I learned how one glorious morning…from Andre Watts.

Questions for Reflection

1. What is one of the best surprises of your life? What did you feel? Was it a spiritual experience for you?

2. If you could do one thing this week to live more deeply, what would it be?

3. If you had to point to some event in the world this week claiming it as a sign of God's activity, what would that event be?

5

How Does Prayer
Really Work?

Scripture Text—Luke 11:1–13

He was praying in a certain place, and after he had finished, one of his disciples said to him, "Lord, teach us to pray, as John taught his disciples." He said to them, "When you pray, say: Father, hallowed be your name. Your kingdom come. Give us each day our daily bread. And forgive us our sins, for we ourselves forgive everyone indebted to us. And do not bring us to the time of trial." And he said to them, "Suppose one of you has a friend, and you go to him at midnight and say to him, 'Friend, lend me three loaves of bread; for a friend of mine has arrived, and I have nothing to set before him.' And he answers from within, 'Do not bother me; the door has already been locked, and my children are with me in bed; I cannot get up and give you anything.' I tell you, even though he will not get up and give him anything because he is his friend, at least because of his persistence he will get up and give him whatever he needs. So I say to you, Ask, and it will be given you; search, and you will find; knock, and the door will be opened for you. For everyone who asks receives, and everyone who searches finds, and for everyone who knocks, the door will be opened. Is there anyone among you who, if your child asks for a fish, will give a snake instead of a fish? Or if the child asks for an egg, will give a scorpion? If you then, who are evil, know how to give good gifts to your children, how much more will the heavenly Father give the Holy Spirit to those who ask him!"

Biblical Reflections

I love this reading from the Gospel of Luke, partly because it offers an insight into Jesus, but also because it gives insight into human experience. Like the early followers, we many times want from Jesus the quick answer, the easy response, the packaged formula—*Five Quick Steps to a Deep Faith*. It can't happen now, and Jesus knew that it couldn't happen then either. Faith and prayer open mysteriously inside us like a flower coming into full blossom.

The scripture story ends with a reference to the Holy Spirit. Luke emphasizes the shaping and transforming role of the Spirit in the lives of Christians. The Holy Spirit is God's energy and creativity, God's most intimate presence. The link to prayer is unmistakable. To pray is to experience the Spirit. The Lord's Prayer (read Matthew's version, and it is significantly different) is important to be sure. Especially is this true for the church receiving this Gospel of Luke. All the words in the prayer point to the coming of the reign of God in the world. Nevertheless, more important than the literal words found in the prayer are the living concepts underneath the skin of the prayer.

The real way to make a connection with this text and prayer is quite simple. Instead of studying about prayer, try for a one-month period to pray daily. Even if it is only five or ten minutes a day, try praying. See how transforming it can be. Notice how you begin to change. Be aware of how God begins to work and grow inside you. That difference will be the activity of the Holy Spirit.

Sermon Text

What intrigues me most about this scripture reading from the Gospel of Luke is the question, the very beginning request of the early disciples.

Jesus had been praying. A point not to be lost. It's one thing to study about the faith, teach the faith in seminary, preach the faith in church, but none of that is a substitute for a daily practice of the faith. Jesus was experiencing prayer, and after he punctuated his prayer with a final amen, these observing disciples ran to him and said, "Lord, teach us to pray, as John taught his disciples."

Fascinating! Evidently John the Baptist had given his followers a distinctive prayer, the kind of prayer that identified them as disciples of John, that embodied the rough-hewn theology of the man who ate locusts and honey in the desert. Could it be that this prayer had became something like a religious tattoo, a kind of personal statement scrawled across the arm that would say to everyone within earshot, "We're associated with

John the Baptist!"? Could it be that this prayer had become a pragmatic identification badge, a bumper sticker attached to their religious life?

It's interesting that people have their distinctive prayers. I've attended enough ecumenical gatherings at this point in my life that I can spot a mile away the Episcopal priest pulling out the Book of Common Prayer or notice the stately formality of the Presbyterian minister as he speaks with that lovely stained-glass voice. Or I can identify the intense ramblings of the Pentecostal minister, making all the mainline ministers very nervous. And, yes, I can tell the Baptists—they pray longer than anyone. You see, what we pray and how we pray says a lot about us.

Well, these early disciples ran to Jesus, and they wanted something that would work. "Give us a prayer like John! C'mon Jesus, let's go down to the tattoo parlor. Give us a prayer that will show everyone that we are your followers."

But do you see what they're doing? They are trying to reduce prayer to some kind of quick-and-easy formula, a one-two-three approach. They want to turn prayer into a bumper sticker—not to release their deepest passion for God, but to hide from their deepest fears in life. And that happens with religion. Some of us use religion as a hole to hide in, but that's never been the purpose of religion. Real faith should become a launching pad from which to really live life! And if you ever have a part of you that wants the church to give you all the simple answers for a complex world, be clear, that's not your faith speaking. That's your fear speaking. These disciples wanted the bumper sticker, tattoo version of prayer.

Notice, to them, Jesus does a masterful thing. He gives them a prayer. "Father, hallowed be your name. Your kingdom come. Give us each day our daily bread." It's a marvelous prayer, the Lord's Prayer. It's a defining prayer. We say it each week in this church. It's as if Jesus is saying to the disciples, "If you need a little prayer to hang on to, fine, use this one. It's simple, but it captures what I'm all about." Jesus gives them a prayer.

But then, in extraordinary fashion, Jesus begins offering the disciples a theology. Theology is not a bad word. Theology is an orientation, an insight about God. Jesus accommodates the disciples, slightly, and gives them the answer they want—they walk away with a prayer in their hip pocket—but then he moves them to a deeper place of understanding and, in fact, gives them two pictures of God.

The first picture is of you sitting at home in your La-Z-Boy, watching television, finishing up the *Dave Letterman* show, maybe getting ready to flip the channels and watch *Late Night with Conan O'Brien*. For the intellectuals, you're watching *Nightline*, no doubt. But you hear the doorbell ring. Startled, you go to the door and look out the window. You can't believe it. Your old college roommate is there. Not only is he there, so is his wife and so are their four kids, all under the age of ten. You open the door, and the real drama begins to unfold. "Hey buddy, we're on vacation. Thought we might come by and surprise you. In fact, thought we might stay for a few days."

What do you do? You let them in, of course, and then you head to the kitchen, only to discover that there's nothing to eat. Your only option seems to be to go to the neighbor across the street and borrow a loaf of bread, some milk, maybe a little lunch meat. You ring the doorbell. No answer. You knock on the door. Still no answer. You peck on the bedroom window. You know they're home. Finally, a porch light comes on, a door opens, and, mustering up all the charm you can, you ask, "Oh, were you asleep?" Your neighbor mutters something. You don't catch it all, but that's probably best. You launch into the explanation. "Company. Unexpected. Four kids. Any milk? Any bread? Any lunch meat?" Although annoyed and irritated, put out and put off, this neighbor finally responds with a grocery sack from the kitchen.

Now, if you don't like that picture, Jesus creates another scene. This time a child, riding in the front seat of the car, says to her mom, "Hey, I deserve a break today! Let's stop at McDonald's for a Happy Meal." What does that mom do? How does that mom respond? Do you think that mom would give the child a scorpion sandwich? Do you think that mom would serve up a poisonous rattlesnake? (I know, people in Texas eat rattlesnakes, but it's just a story. Work with me here!) The answer is so obvious that the question becomes rhetorical. Jesus knows that the essence of any good parent is being responsive to the requests of children.

In both stories, Jesus is trying to drive home the central essence of how prayer *really* works. His theological point is found in the last verse of the reading: *If you then, who are evil, know how to give good gifts to your children, how much more will the heavenly Father give the Holy Spirit to those who ask him!* That is to say, if we as human beings, with all our limitations and irritations, know how to respond to neighbors and children, how much more does God know how to respond to our prayers. And, in the end, there is one response to all our prayers. Finally only one—that God gives us the gift of the Holy Spirit.

I daresay that most of us have had the idea that prayer is our way of getting things from God. At least that's the orientation to prayer that I got while growing up in the church. How it works is that God is "up there" and I am "down here." When I pray, it's like sending a FAX message to God. In this way, prayer becomes, primarily, my way of communicating to God what I want, what I need, what I feel. That's why most of us only think about prayer when we're in trouble, when we really need something from God. Isn't that when most of us pray? But think about it for a minute. Isn't it degrading to any relationship when a child, a spouse, a friend only talks to us when they want something from us?

Yet, for me, in this childhood view of God it was always perplexing how God answered my prayers. Has that ever been perplexing to you? Because what I found is that sometimes it seemed as if God had answered my prayers. At other times, it seemed that God had ignored my prayers. But it really got confusing when I thought God had answered my prayers, but it turned out that things were worse than before I even prayed. So then I prayed for God to undo the previous prayer! Confusing? Very confusing.

Confusing until I really started seeing something here in this scripture reading. As a child my orientation to prayer was little more than putting in my order to God, sort of like a trip to the heavenly Service Merchandise, waiting for the answer to roll down to the showroom floor. But in this reading, I started to see that the point of asking and searching and knocking is not so much to get things from God, but to be in relationship with God. That's why Jesus says when we pray God will answer with the Holy Spirit. Because what is the Spirit but the most intimate, most relational, most loving presence of God's very being?

I have been at hospitals and I have prayed with people. I have prayed for people to get well. I have prayed for people to be healed. I've even taken a small dab of oil, anointed a person's head, and prayed for that person's well-being. And sometimes after my prayer the person did get well. And I was so thankful. Sometimes after my prayer the person did not get well. And I was sad, sometimes very sad, but I was still thankful. It's not that God answered "yes" in one case and ignored the other. It's not even that God answered "yes" in one case and "no" in another. I think God answered "yes" in both cases. Because what happened in that moment of praying, more than getting something from God, was that I was sharing the presence of God with another human being. And in the stillness of prayer, the Holy Spirit was present with us.

What I've realized over the last few years is that my experience of prayer has gradually switched from the mode of *asking God for favors* to the mode of *listening for the Spirit* when I pray. I pray for others all the time. And I think those prayers make a difference in God and a difference in the world. But most of all, prayer seems to work because it makes such a difference in me. That's why when I have a problem, I pray to God. It's not usually the case that the problem suddenly vanishes when I'm finished praying. But what happens is that I now see the problem differently or I find I have the inner resources to face the problem or I remember again that my companionship with God will see me through whatever it is I need to face. That's how the Spirit answers my prayer. Here, every week, I pray for people who have deep losses in their lives. When I finish my prayer, their loss is still real, but somehow the Spirit connects me with them, and in that sacred moment God's healing works. It's an answer to prayer.

I read a moving story about prayer as listening a couple of years ago in Sam Keen's book *Hymns to An Unknown God.* What he discovered was the miracle of stillness. Listen to his personal story:

> In 1972, I was living alone in an apartment on Telegraph Hill in San Francisco, divorced after seventeen years of marriage and at the end of a love affair. My children were living a thousand miles away. My days were filled with emptiness and yearning.... When night came to the city hungry ghosts and angry furies came out of the woodwork and wandered around my sparse bachelor apartment in search of my soul. They whispered, "The best of your life is past. You have made too many mistakes, hurt too many people. You can't start again".... When I had endured as much of their maddening abuse as I could stand, I left the apartment and began a long evening of wandering through the city.... I don't remember how many nights I ran from madness and pain. I do remember the moment at about two a.m. near Pier 32 when I finally had had enough and resolved that I would stop running.... I walked home.

Keen goes on to talk about arriving back at his apartment and designating a particular chair in his living room, a prayer chair really. There he vowed to sit and pray and be still and face his fears. And although chaos might swirl around his life, there he would sit and listen. In that chair, he would sit with the deepest of divine stillness. That's how prayer *really* works.

I wish I could tell you that it's as easy as calling in an order on the Home Shopping Network. But it's not. It's better than that. Prayer works because we are in relationship with the one who is the perfect neighbor and the perfect parent, who gives us something better than things, who gives us God's very self. No wonder Henri Nouwen would end his book *With Open Hands* by summarizing that "praying is living." Yes, praying is a new way to live! That's really what the early disciples most needed. It's what we need, too.

Questions for Reflection

1. What has been your basic understanding of prayer?

2. Have you ever felt God's presence during or after you've prayed?

3. In what way can all of life become an act of praying?

6

The Declaration of the Divine Child

Scripture Text—Mark 1:4–11

John the baptizer appeared in the wilderness, proclaiming a baptism of repentance for the forgiveness of sins. And people from the whole Judean countryside and all the people of Jerusalem were going out to him, and were baptized by him in the river Jordan, confessing their sins. Now John was clothed with camel's hair, with a leather belt around his waist, and he ate locusts and wild honey. He proclaimed, "The one who is more powerful than I is coming after me; I am not worthy to stoop down and untie the thong of his sandals. I have baptized you with water; but he will baptize you with the Holy Spirit." In those days Jesus came from Nazareth of Galilee and was baptized by John in the Jordan. And just as he was coming up out of the water, he saw the heavens torn apart and the Spirit descending like a dove on him. And a voice came from heaven, "You are my son, the Beloved; with you I am well pleased."

Biblical Reflections

The baptism of Jesus has traditionally been something of an embarrassment to the church. On the one hand, to say that Jesus was baptized as a mere example for his followers that they should be baptized is not to say enough. At the same time, to say that Jesus was baptized because he had committed sins that needed forgiving probably says too much. Nevertheless, here it is in the scripture text of the Gospel of Mark.

What I suggest in the sermon is that Jesus was baptized because in the ritual experience of the event he was seeking a firsthand, living, immediate experience of the divine. In this soulful moment of baptism, Jesus is demonstrating his soulful yearning for God. Not as a didactic example for others to follow, though that's certainly present, but because in his own journey he desired depth and meaning for his living. Rather than being exempt from the spiritual quest, Jesus is the quintessential example of a person on the quest for God.

I like this idea because it points me on the journey of faith. Faith is not just becoming plugged into the institutional church. In reality, many are connected to the institutional church but never experience spiritual transformation. Jesus valued spiritual transformation more than anything— his own and the transformation of others. In this sense, the baptism of Jesus becomes his way of giving us a map for the journey. Not that he can live the journey for us, but he can indicate what is most important on the journey. This is obviously a far cry from the idea that seems to exist in so many churches, namely, if we get people baptized, then that's enough. It has never been enough. Not for Jesus. Not for us.

This story of his baptism, like so many others in the life of Jesus, reminds me that more than affirming that "this once happened to Jesus," I must ask myself, How can this now happen to me? What does it mean for me to experience birth, baptism, wilderness, crucifixion, resurrection? For the Jesus story to become our story, there must be an intimate sharing with the deepest spiritual realities that Jesus experienced. Therefore, I encourage you as you read the Gospels to ask yourself the existential question, Where am I in the story?

Sermon Text

This particular reading in the Gospel of Mark is embarrassing. At least it was embarrassing in the life of the early church. Clearly Mark portrays John the Baptist as a desert preacher calling people to repent of their sins. But more than preaching, John also performed the ritual of baptism. He would go down to the river Jordan, shed that burlap sack of a sport coat, wade into the waters of the river, and perform "a baptism of repentance for the forgiveness of sins."

In that ritual of desert baptism, people would denounce their past. People would revel in forgiveness. People would live in a new God-oriented direction. People would anticipate their participation in the kingdom of God. And all of that was fine and good until that one day when Jesus showed up. It was Jesus, the one the church confessed as Lord and Savior, it was Jesus coming forward during the invitation hymn, it was Jesus standing in front of John the Baptist saying, "I, too, need to be baptized."

Do you see why that would have been a little uncomfortable, if not embarrassing, to the early church? Why would Jesus—sinless Jesus, innocent Jesus, Son of God Jesus—why would Jesus need to be baptized? Matthew, writing after Mark, was so troubled by it that he even offered a few theological explanations. This is why Matthew's version is different from Mark's. Luke softens the story even more. But not Mark. Instead, what you find in Mark's Gospel is this straightforward need of Jesus to be baptized. But why? Why is Jesus baptized?

I think there's something very significant and deep for us here today. On the one hand, I look at this baptism, and it becomes a symbolic ritual moment of transformation for Jesus. And please don't misunderstand me. When I say the words *symbolic* and *ritual,* those are words full and rich and ripe. He goes down into the water, the heavens open up, the Spirit of God descends like a dove, and the word that comes from God is: "You are my Son, the Beloved; with you I am well pleased."

And what I hear in that declaration is an exuberant expression of relationship. Two metaphors for his relationship with God are really offered. Jesus is in relationship to God as a child is in relationship to a parent. Be careful not to read too much gender into this baptismal moment. The declaration is not about the maleness of Jesus, that is, he's a son. It is about the relationship that Jesus has to the divine being, and the metaphor that is used is child and parent. It's not the only metaphor that a person could use to describe the relationship between God and Jesus, but it's certainly a good one.

For Jesus to know and feel himself as close to God as a child is to a parent was and is an incredibly powerful moment. Now, I'll tell you when you see this metaphor come to life. Every single time one of our children's choirs sings, you should see how the parents and grandparents in this church behave. Were you here at the early Christmas Eve service? There were more video cameras running, more camera flashes popping, more necks craning than I've ever seen in my life. These children got more attention than if the Dallas Cowboys had made it to the Super Bowl!

Now, some might look at that liturgical paparazzi and think *how irreverent.* But I don't look at it that way. Yes, you can go overboard, but what I hope is that every child in that choir had a parent or a grandparent or a guardian who was there just to watch him, hear her, there because they value that child so deeply. Because what I know, what you know too, is that the problem with children in our culture is not that they are overvalued, but undervalued. Children can't get too much affirmation. They can't get too much love. They can't get too much attention. Now, they can get the wrong kind of attention, but they can never get too much of the right kind of parental relationship.

At his baptism, Jesus has a moment of spiritual closeness to God, and at that moment he feels like a child feels with a mother or a father or a grandparent. And it is out of that closeness of relationship that Jesus would share the good news of God and, in fact, would even offer that same child-parent closeness to people he would meet in ancient Palestine. Jesus would say to people, "When you pray to God, just go ahead and call God, Abba, Papa, Dad, Daddy." Again, it's not the maleness of the word that matters the most, but the relationship Jesus gives as a gift. And that gift emerged out of his own baptismal experience.

The other metaphor found in this baptismal declaration is that Jesus was beloved. Please don't read some kind of lurid quality into that word beloved. It's unfortunate that the word "lover" has taken on some kind of promiscuous, seedy, shady connotation. To have a lover or to be the beloved of another human being is one of the most alive, most awakening, most intimate experiences we'll ever have. This is why frequently in the Bible, in both Old and New Testaments, God is compared to a bride, a groom, a lover. If you can think of a moment in your life when you really felt alive with love toward another human being, then you've begun to understand what it's like to be in relationship with God.

In his prayer journal *Sacraments of Love*, Father Andrew Greeley begins almost every prayer with the expression—"My Love…." In his novels Greeley has explicitly played with the image of the lover. Some have criticized this priest for using the lover image, but what Greeley knows, even as a priest, is that to incorporate the divine into our lives through the metaphor of beloved is one of the most transformative experiences we'll ever have.

Sometimes I think we fall into a rut by addressing God only as "Dear Heavenly Father." There's nothing wrong with that. I use that at times, too. But wouldn't it be refreshing to occasionally pray, "O God My Love." What a tender, exciting, almost breathtaking way of thinking about God. The mystic Hildegard of Bingen once wrote that the "soul is kissed by God." That's a nice lover image. Another mystic, Meister Eckhart, once wrote, "God is voluptuous and delicious." Isn't that a beautiful lover image?

At his baptism, Jesus experiences this intense moment of God awareness. God lives with him as a parent lives with a child. God lives with him as a lover lives with her beloved. This story obviously says something about Jesus. At the same time, this story of Jesus' baptism says something about us. I had never thought about this until recently, but there are two moments that become moments of grace in this church. One is when I hold a baby in my arms for a service of blessing. And that moment is so powerful for the entire church because we long to be held by God in this way. Another moment is a wedding, that incredible moment when the groom waits and the bride walks down that long, long, long center aisle. And that moment is so awesome because we all long to find God as a lover.

What I observe is that there is in our culture a pervasive hunger for parent. I see this in little children. In teenagers. I even see it in adults. It's a hunger to be in relationship to an older man or an older woman who can provide the energy of mothering or fathering.

I saw this about a year ago when I finished a round of golf with one of my good friends. We went into the clubhouse to have lunch; the talk was mostly about work, church, family. You know, trying to put a positive spin on our golf game. But then one thing led to another, and he started talking about his father. He said, "You know, when my father and I get together it feels as if there's something missing. I don't really know what it is, but it's something." And then I looked up and saw tears welling up around his eyes, and he said, "You know, I just wish he would tell me that he's proud of me." Folks, this is a thirty-nine-year-old man who has one of the most responsible corporate positions in the city of Atlanta, and he's starving for some kind of parent energy.

No wonder someone like singer Van Morrison sings of the pain of feeling like a motherless or fatherless child, that feeling of being a long, long way from any sense of home. Sometimes we do feel that way, lost, alone, orphaned, don't we? Friends, very few of us ever get everything we want from our earthly mothers or fathers. Some of us had really fine parents. Others had abusive, angry, almost deplorable parents. And probably all of us have some childhood issue we need to clarify as we become adults. Most of us, maybe not all of us, but most of us need to work at self-understanding rather than blaming our parents.

But my, we do—both parents and children—know how to push each other's buttons. Someone told me a joke a few weeks ago, at least I think it was a joke, about the man who called his retired mother in Florida.

He said, "How are you doing, Mother?" She said, "Not so good. I feel very weak." "Well, why do you feel so weak, Mother?" She said, "Well, I haven't eaten in thirty-eight days." The son, aghast, said to her, "Mother, why haven't you eaten in thirty-eight days?" His mother replied, "Because I didn't want my mouth filled with food when you called."

Nothing like a little motherly guilt, right?

What I've concluded is that almost all of us long for mother energy, father energy, and that longing is really a spiritual longing that is deep within our souls. I didn't have to ask my golfing buddy any questions. I understood exactly what he was talking about. But I also know he's probably never going to get exactly what he needs from his earthly dad. He can try. And I encouraged him to try. Yet, just as Jesus found his God awareness in the relationship of parent and child, so we, too, must finally find our closeness with God at that point. You and I, not just Jesus, but all of us in this sanctuary this morning need to hear God say to us, "You are my son. You are my daughter. You are my child." This is why Paul would say in the book of Galatians, "In Christ Jesus you are all children of God" (3:26).

You see, when we live with that awareness, we know that no matter what we go through in life we are never alone because a good parent never abandons a child. And God doesn't abandon you. And what that also means is that when our identity becomes that of a child of God, we can start to live with confidence because this world becomes a gift to be enjoyed. And when we are really declared a child of God, we can treat other people as if they, too, are God's children, because we don't have to show them up or belittle them. We don't have to be afraid of them because we know there's enough divine love for all people. Here's a radical idea. When our daily identity becomes child of God, we can even start to see the beautiful potential in other people.

Let me tell you what surprised me most about my first Boar's Head and Yule Log Festival we have here each year at University Church. I knew what was coming. I knew the choir would sing and the musicians would play. I knew the doors of the triptych would be opened. And I knew that a mother and father would hold up a baby Jesus. I knew it was coming. But when those doors opened, I found myself spiritually moved by seeing this baby held up to the congregation. Held up to God. I felt this lump in my throat about the size of a Texas grapefruit. But I said to myself, "Oh, it's just because this is the first time you've seen it." But then it happened again at 5:00 p.m. Then again on Sunday. And then one more time. And it happened because there is a part of all of us that not only admires that baby, but a part of us that is that baby. God declares, God holds each and every one of us up, and says, "My son. My daughter. My child."

And don't you see that just as we long for the divine parent, we also long for the divine lover? Jesus was declared beloved, but we all want to feel ourselves beloved of God. This is why romantic love is one of the most religious experiences we'll ever have. But what most of us fail to understand is that the divine lover is not found in marrying the most beautiful girl or the most handsome man in the senior class. The divine lover is not found in the glossy images of magazines or in the sparkling personalities of movie stars. Nor is the divine lover found moving from relationship to relationship to relationship every time the newness wears off.

The reality is that I cannot be everything for my wife. I know it's hard to believe, but it's true! And she can't be everything for my life. Again, hard to believe but true! We are beloved to each other, but finally there is a spiritual longing for love and intimacy and acceptance that only God can provide. And we find it in prayer. We find it in worship. We find it in contemplation. We find it in service. You see, our soul is only at home when it's in the arms of the lover, God.

In many ways, the early church had it all wrong about the baptism of Jesus. The fact that Jesus was baptized isn't meant to be an embarrassing commentary on his personal need of repentance or confession. His baptism is a sign that he wanted to be close to God, to touch the transcendent, the numinous, to feel the mystery of relationship with God. And you see, that's finally what we want to touch, too. To be in relationship with God so that we are safe like a child in God's arms. Or we are secure like a lover in God's heart. There's nothing embarrassing about that.

Questions for Reflection

1. Can you name one of the most intense spiritual longings you've ever experienced?

2. Often like a basketball coach, we bring in substitutes for our spiritual longings. What substitutes have you masterfully used in your life?

3. Do you recall your own baptism? What does it mean to you that you have been baptized?

SECTION II

Recognition

7

Dancing the
Dance of Gratitude

Scripture Text—Luke 17:11–19

On the way to Jerusalem Jesus was going through the region between Samaria and Galilee. As he entered a village, ten lepers approached him. Keeping their distance, they called out, saying, "Jesus, Master, have mercy on us!" When he saw them, he said to them, "Go and show yourselves to the priests." And as they went, they were made clean. Then one of them, when he saw that he was healed, turned back, praising God with a loud voice. He prostrated himself at Jesus' feet and thanked him. And he was a Samaritan. Then Jesus asked, "Were not ten made clean? But the other nine, where are they? Was none of them found to return and give praise to God except this foreigner?" Then he said to him, "Get up and go on your way; your faith has made you well."

Biblical Reflections

Part of the challenge of this text is that it is so familiar. It's like telling a joke and everyone knows the punch line. If you attended Sunday school as a child, you can recall the pictures taped to the wall in your classroom. Familiarity can easily become cliche. Yet, despite the familiarity, I love this reading because it touches the heart of what it means to be alive, namely, being grateful.

In my own life experience, I find that I am most deeply connected to God and others when I am most open to the experience of gratitude. I wanted to take this story, obviously meant to encourage gratitude, and then connect it to the traditional American holiday of Thanksgiving. That's part of the background of the sermon. That's more challenging than you might think, given the fact that the holidays are always a mixed bag for the congregation. Some have cherished memories and wonderful plans, while for others the holidays signal pain, disappointment, and loss.

Rather than condemning the lepers who did not come back, I found myself intrigued with the one who did come back; moreover, the one who was so moved by his experience with God that he could do nothing but come back and express his gratitude and joy. It's this experience of being at home, at one with God, at peace, an experience of having a glimpse into the presence of God that moves me in the text. This scripture text invites each of us to open up, spread wide our arms, tune up our senses, and finally live with the joy and anticipation of the presence of God in our lives.

Sermon Text

This morning I want you to see a small cafe in London. The buildings are old. The air is heavy. Sitting alone at one of the tables is the great Irish poet William Butler Yeats. It is his fiftieth birthday. He sits there in the midst of noise and chatter; the hustle and bustle of people surround him. But while he sits there something remarkable happens, happens only briefly, but happens in such a way that he will never be the same again. You can call it an "epiphany," a "peak" moment of experience. You might even call it a "religious" experience, but however you name it and whatever you call it, his life would never be the same again.

Listen to his words:

> My fiftieth year had come and gone,
> I sat, a solitary man,
> In a crowded London shop,
> An open book and empty cup
> On the marble table-top.
>
> While on the shop and street I gazed
> My body of a sudden blazed;
> And twenty minutes more or less
> It seemed, so great my happiness,
> That I was blessed and could bless.

Marvelous. Absolutely marvelous. For a moment time ceased to be time, and in this peak moment of experience he had this intense flow of life, a moment of blessing, of gratefulness, a moment when the feeling of thanksgiving bubbled up inside his soul like champagne, and all he could do was experience this largesse quality of life.

I know it's not traditional, but could it be that this man, this table, this blazing moment of blessedness and blessing could become for us a symbol of the holiday we call Thanksgiving? I don't want to replace the turkey and dressing. Don't forget the cranberry sauce. Pumpkin pie, too. I love the whole picture of an American Thanksgiving, but could it be that this day we spend with family and friends, this day of food and football, could become something more for us, become a day when we recognize that God has both blessed and called us to bless?

It was a remarkable moment of blessing that took place on that road with Jesus long ago. The geography that Luke notes is more theological than historical. Jesus is in Samaria, and the fact that he is in Samaria tells you that he is in foreign territory. Jesus walks down the road and sees ten lepers approaching him. The fact that he sees them at all is something of a miracle. These were the invisible people of the first century. As Samaritans they were marginalized from mainstream Judaism, and as lepers they were considered religiously unclean. Nobody wanted to see a leper, touch a leper, hear a leper. In fact, when they walked down the dusty streets of the little villages they were required to call out, "Leper! Unclean! Leper!" And everybody with money and health and happiness scattered, because nobody wanted to be close to a leper.

Not only does Jesus see one, he sees ten of them. There they are, positioned at the corner, ready for another day of holding out their begging cups for donations. As Jesus passes by they call out to him, "Jesus, Master, have mercy on us!" Feel the desperation this morning. Hear the shrillness of the voice. "Have mercy on us!" Do you feel the isolation, the loneliness, the shame, the unacceptability of the cry? They had been victims for so long that it would have been tempting not to have cried out, to just assume that Jesus, like all the others, wanted to walk on by. What do you do when you see a homeless man? Turn away? Cross the street? Divert your eyes? These lepers, these begging lepers, these desperate lepers, they call out to Jesus. Do you feel the indignity of their lives?

How many lines do you have to stand in; how many times does some government bureaucrat have to tell you that you're in the wrong office; how many hours do you have to wait in an emergency room before you lose all energy to cry out? How many arguments does a marriage have to endure; how many times do you have to be passed over for the promotion; how many times do you have to visit the school because your teenager is in trouble again; how many times before you no longer have the energy to cry out? I might as well ask it this morning: What cry is inside of you that you need to offer to God this day? What cry do you bring to church this morning?

You know, there's one part of church that I don't really like. It's that part that seems to require that we have to clean up before we come here on Sunday morning. I'm not talking about baths and showers and what you wear to church. (Well, the baths and showers are much appreciated.) But it's that expectation that seems to say you have to clean up your spiritual life, emotional life, psychological life before you can really be here. It's that feeling that somehow my problems or people like me aren't really welcome here.

I don't know. But what I do know is that there is no human cry that goes unheard by God. It's not the case that our prayers are like putting two quarters in a God machine, and we get exactly what we order, Coke or Dr. Pepper. It's not that simple. But take from this story what it will give you this morning. There is no cry in your life that God does not hear, does not feel, does not experience in God's own being. And by the way, that also means that there is no human cry unwelcome in the church that belongs to God. And so even though no one else wanted to listen to these lepers, Jesus listened. And the fact that he listened at all tells us something profoundly true about God.

"Have mercy on us!" they cried.

"Mercy? Sure, I'll give you some mercy," says Jesus. "Go show yourselves to the priest. Go pick up your certificates of cleanliness. Mercy, sure, I specialize in bringing people back to life with mercy!"

And they went. All ten of them. But there was one, just one of them who looked at his hands, his feet, the skin on his arms, and for the first time in years he felt well, looked like himself. And in one brief, remarkable moment, there was a blaze of well-being that came to him as a gift of God. He wheeled around. Danced with delight. He praised God in a loud voice. This was no time to be quiet. Forget good manners. Breathlessly he ran back to Jesus—why, he hadn't run in years—threw himself down on the ground, and said, "Thank you."

Sure, Jesus asks about the other nine, but he knows that, really, there's no explaining it. I can't explain it. I don't know where they are, what they're doing, why they could not take time to say thank you. I don't know a lot of things. I don't know how some people can live in a nice home, have a nice family, have a nice career—I mean, I don't know how some people—how I—can some days still be unhappy with all of that. I don't know how someone can be a member of this church that is so obviously filled with talent and joy and compassion and spirit and still be unhappy. I don't know. I don't know.

Jesus says to this man, "Get up, and go now. You have found the essence of faith, and that faith now makes you a whole person. Come on, live your life."

I suspect that none of us is ever whole until we reach such a moment, that moment when we clearly see we have been both blessed by God and are called to bless.

In his new book *The Longing for Home,* Fred Buechner talks about what he calls "the great dance" of joy. He recalls a family vacation to Sea World in Florida and how he and his wife were so amazed by the grace and beauty of the great whales' breaking the surface of the water that they were moved to tears. Buechner writes:

> We shed tears because we were given a glimpse of the Peaceable Kingdom, and it had almost broken our hearts. For a few moments we had seen Eden and been part of the great dance that goes on at the heart of creation. We shed tears because we were given a glimpse of the way life was created to be....The world does bad things to us all, and we do bad things to the world and to each other and maybe most of all to ourselves, but in that dazzle of bright water as the glittering whales hurled themselves into the sun, I believe that what we saw was that joy is what we belong to....God's joy is in our blood.

What Frederick Buechner discovered at that touristy place called Sea World is exactly what W. B. Yeats discovered in that London cafe. And it's also what that pathetic, desperate, begging leper discovered in that little village outside Jerusalem, namely, that we are only whole when we learn how to dance the dance of joy, of gratitude, of amazement. And in that dance we not only receive from God, but we also give back to God.

You know what I think happens to a lot of us? Sometimes I think we look at gratitude as something we will have "one of these days." One of these days when I get out of school, one of these days when I meet the right person, one of these days when I get the right job, one of these days when I can live in the right house, one of these days when I finally get to retire...then, when that happens, then I will dance the dance of gratitude! The trouble is that every time you get right up to the moment of being thankful, you always find one more condition upon which you want to base your gratitude, and the wholeness we want eludes us again.

Look at it like this: Every person in this sanctuary this morning would like to be a little happier. Go ahead, look around today. Look at the person sitting next to you. Look at the person sitting in the pew right in front of you. It's okay to look at the humanity that fills this place Sunday after Sunday. I think every one of us would like to be a bit happier. And I think every one of us would like to have a good Thanksgiving Day this week. Happy. Healthy. Experiencing life with the deepest of satisfaction. All of us would like that.

But the ones who finally find it are the ones who learn how to open their lives to it and the ones who learn how to give thanks for it. As strange as it may sound, we have to give thanks before we can find the wholeness that will make us thankful. Because if we wait until everything in life is lined up perfectly, we will never be thankful, and we will never be whole, and we will never be happy.

Have you ever noticed that almost every family has a disaster story about a Thanksgiving turkey? You know, stories of the turkey catching fire—*that's turkey flambe*. Stories of the family dog getting hold of the turkey right before dinner—*that's turkey caninus*. Stories of putting the turkey in the oven but forgetting to turn it on—*that's turkey in the raw*, not to be confused with *turkey in the straw*. Stories of baking the turkey but forgetting to pull out the wrapped turkey parts inside the turkey—*that's turkey odoriferous*.

We all could share our stories of less-than-perfect Thanksgivings. But if perfection, whether personal, family, church, or world is required for our feeling of thanksgiving, we will never give thanks. That means we will never be whole. That means we will never dance the dance of gratitude. Perfection never happens, but epiphanies and peeks and glimpses and insights of gratefulness do.

My hope is that not only this week, but every week, you can take the holiday of Thanksgiving and turn it into both a noun and a verb. Thanksgiving is what you receive from God—noun. Thanksgiving is what you offer to God and others—verb. Or, if you like the image of that little London shop, I hope you find a blazing twenty minutes when you know yourself as both blessed and able to bless.

Questions for Reflection

1. Can you name a "religious" experience in your life?

2. Have you ever felt a deep sense of gratitude? When? What were the circumstances?

3. When have you felt the deepest need to ask God for mercy?

8

What Are You
Afraid Of?

Scripture Text—Mark 4:35–41

On that day, when evening had come, he said to them, "Let us go across to the other side." And leaving the crowd behind, they took him with them in the boat, just as he was. Other boats were with him. A great windstorm arose, and the waves beat into the boat, so that the boat was already being swamped. But he was in the stern, asleep on the cushion; and they woke him up and said to him, "Teacher, do you not care that we are perishing?" He woke up and rebuked the wind, and said to the sea, "Peace! Be still!" Then the wind ceased, and there was a dead calm. He said to them, "Why are you afraid? Have you still no faith?" And they were filled with great awe and said to one another, "Who then is this, that even the wind and the sea obey him?"

Biblical Reflections

This is one of the most interesting readings in the New Testament in that Matthew, Mark, and Luke all have some version of it. To compare the three stories in a synoptic version of the Gospels is interesting and insightful. In fact, this reading was used several years ago in New Testament studies to demonstrate that each of the Gospel writers was writing for a specific situation with a specific theological purpose.

It's important to appreciate that Mark was writing to a particular audience, with particular concerns, and is offering a particular theological viewpoint. To put the Gospels into the blender and make them tell one story is a mistake. Mark, like any good minister, was trying to address his situation, a situation that might be described as a church under intense scrutiny and persecution. The Roman government had turned the heat up on the church. Some were being persecuted, others martyred. All, no doubt, were coping with fear. When these earliest Christians came to faith in Jesus Christ, none of them had bargained for this kind of experience. They were all coming to terms with what it means to wait, even wait for the coming of the Lord in the midst of stormy circumstances.

It is this question of how to wait, to live, to find courage in life that I connect to the sermon. We all have storms. We all have fear. We all need courage. In the sermon, I try to acknowledge our stormy existence, as well as offering a word of encouragement and hope for people to really live their lives. What I find more and more is that people need to be set free! This is exactly what Jesus did for the early disciples. There is, after all, nothing that imprisons our life more than our fears. To find courage to live is what this story is all about.

Sermon Text

In his book *The Active Life*, Parker Palmer tells about the time when he was in his early forties and facing some of the demons that go along with that age. He decided to go on an Outward Bound experience. Everything was going along pretty well until he reached that moment when they hooked his body to a harness and told him to lean it out over a mountain cliff. Listen to his words:

> I remember the cliff too well. It started with a five-foot drop to a small ledge, then a ten-foot drop to another ledge, then a third and final drop all the way down. I tried to negotiate the first drop; my feet instantly went out from under me, and I fell heavily to the first ledge.
>
> "I don't think you quite have it yet," the instructor observed astutely. "You are leaning too close to the rock face. You need to lean much farther back so your feet will grip the wall."
>
> That advice went against my every instinct. Surely one should hug the wall, not lean out over the void! But on the second drop I tried to lean back; better, but not far enough, and I hit the second ledge with a thud not unlike the first.
>
> "You still don't have it," said the ever-observant instructor. "Try again."
>
> Since my next try would be the last one, her counsel was not especially comforting. But try I did, and much to my amazement I found myself moving slowly down the rock wall. Step by step I

made my way with growing confidence until, about halfway down, I suddenly realized that I was heading toward a very large hole in the rock, and—not knowing anything better to do—I froze. The instructor waited a small eternity for me to thaw out, and when she realized that I was showing no signs of life she yelled up, "Is anything wrong, Parker?" as if she needed to ask. To this day I do not know the source of the childlike voice that came up from within me, but my response is a matter of public record: "I don't want to talk about it."

The instructor yelled back, "Then I think it's time you learned the Outward Bound motto." Wonderful, I thought. I am about to die, and she is feeding me bromides. But then she spoke words I have never forgotten, words so true that they empowered me to negotiate the rest of the cliff without incident. She said, *If you can't get out of it, get into it.*

Don't you imagine when that wind started to howl, and those waves started to break, and that boat started to rock, and their stomachs started to roll, don't you imagine that those early disciples wanted to get out of it? And don't you imagine that when that boat started to take on water, and it started to dip down lower and lower into the sea, and when that wooden hull started to creak like the bones of old men, don't you imagine that they wanted to get out of it? You can almost hear the panic in their voices. "Teacher," they cried, "Teacher, don't you care that we're perishing? Aren't you going to do something? Don't let this happen to us!"

The one moment I like best in this reading from Mark's Gospel is the place where Jesus says to the disciples, "Let's cross over to the other side." Crossing over. Before the storm, before the fear, before the challenge, there is the crossing over. The truth is that their lives could have been *storm-free* had they decided *not* to cross over. And the same could be said of Mark's church in the capital city of Rome. This church was under intense pressure from the Roman government. Some had even been put to death. All of the pain and persecution could have been avoided had they decided *not* to cross over into the world of being Christians, just stayed in the secular world of the Roman Empire. But they did cross over. For Jesus, the point of living was never to avoid storms. It was to cross over to the places where he thought God wanted him to live.

And that should be true of us, too.

Think of the many crossings of your life. Going off to college for the first time is a kind of crossing over. Taking a new job in a new city is a kind of crossing over. Becoming a parent for the first time is a kind of life crossing. Having all of your children move out of the house is a kind of crossing. Having all of your children move *back* into the house is a crossing, too. Having to make decisions for an elderly parent is a life crossing, isn't it?

And I must tell you, churches, like people, have to face moments of crossing over. Welcoming a new minister is a significant crossing for a church. But that's nothing compared to the innovation now required of churches that want to reach out to people in today's culture. The reason is that the kind of church many of us have come to love and value is not exactly the same kind of church the culture wants or even needs. The message is the same, but the means of offering the message are changing. And the people out in the culture aren't going to adjust to our ways at the church. Frankly, they're just not going to come. We're the ones who have to love the culture enough and be passionate enough about the message of the good news that we'll do whatever it takes to reach the people out in the culture. And believe me, there is not one Protestant church in America today exempt from facing this cultural crossing. There aren't many brave ones out there making the crossing, but, believe me, every church is facing it.

And with every crossing in our lives, whether it's congregational or individual, there is almost always a storm. I have a friend right now who has worked for the same bank for almost twenty years. Bright. Dedicated. Creative. He's been in line for years to be a vice president. Three years ago the bank was sold. Personnel shifted. Gradually he found himself more and more out of the loop of power. And also more and more unhappy. His wife called Marti last Saturday morning and said, "Well, John decided to take their offer and leave the bank."

Do you feel the ferocity of his stormy crossing? And what would you have said to him last week on the phone about Jesus? Is Jesus with him in this crossing? Is John in the boat alone? Is there some calm that he can count on in the midst of his chaos?

Well, some suggest that all you need to do is pray, give your life to Jesus, and then Jesus will calm all the storms of life. And I want to say that maybe sometimes perhaps that happens. Maybe sometimes God calms storms as quickly as they arise. Dramatically. Instantaneously. Maybe.

But could it be that there is a deeper message of Jesus? The point being not so much that Jesus will rescue us from our storms as it is that Jesus will endure with us in our storms. And if that's the case, the Outward Bound motto is true. *If you can't get out of it, get into it!* The more we get into our storms, and the less we avoid them, and the more courage we find to face them, and the more we try to grow through them, the better our chance is of finding this marvelous, mystical presence of Jesus.

Jesus calmed the storm. "Peace! Be still!" But then he addressed the real issue in that boat, namely, the disciples' fear and anxiety and skittishness, and he invited them to rediscover faith. Faith is not belief that the storm will stop; it's belief that there is One with us whose love is stronger than the storm.

Did you see the movie *Father of the Bride,* starring Steve Martin? I liked the movie, but I especially liked it because I've concluded after performing countless numbers of weddings that the most bewildered person in the entire chaotic drama of the wedding ceremony is the father of the bride. Most fathers of the bride just don't get it. They're clueless. They don't understand why the invitations have to be a certain way, why the bride needs this particular wedding consultant, why only a certain kind of flower will do, why the wedding reception can't be held just anywhere. They don't get it. Furthermore, by the night of the rehearsal this grown man has often been reduced to an automatic teller machine; money just flies out of his pocket!

But in the movie, do you remember what Steve Martin really wants to get out of it? He resists everything that is happening. He can't understand why they have to do everything that "Franz," that offbeat wedding consultant, wants them to do.

But then there is that moment at the end of the wedding, after the reception, after everyone has gone home, that this father of the bride slouches down in a chair utterly exhausted. He stares at all the clutter. His house is a complete wreck. And then, the phone rings. It's his daughter, the bride, calling from the airport. She says, "Dad, I just wanted to call and say thanks for everything, and tell you that I love you."

And at that moment, the storm of money and the chaotic details and the prattle of wedding consultants do not matter. Because the only thing that matters in the storm is knowing someone loves you.

Folks, we can't avoid our storms. Sure, we get afraid. We're not sure what the next crossing will be like. But there are crossings every single day in our lives that we must make. There are mountains each day that we must climb. There are cliffs that we must lean out over and rappel down. To avoid those moments is to avoid the adventure God is calling us to live.

You see, I believe that Jesus does offer us peace. And who knows? Maybe that peace does come like the instant stilling of the storm. But more often than not, that peace blossoms slowly, quietly, imperceptibly, the way a rose opens its petals when kissed by morning light. It's a peace that's always there. A calm that always awaits. A presence that's always available.

One of the most influential figures in my life, Thomas Merton, calls it a "hidden wholeness that lies beneath the surface of our lives." The hidden wholeness. What Jesus wanted the disciples to understand is that God's calm is always just an inch below the surface of the storm. It's there. It's always there. And that's why, instead of running from our storms, we need to find courage to get into our storms because God is there. And that's why even churches can find courage to change and experiment and try and then try again. And if it doesn't work, try yet again. Because no matter how scary the crossing for any church, there is a hidden wholeness of God that is within the church.

Let's face it. Every morning we get up we really face one big question. *Will I live life out of my fear or out of my courage?* And that's not easy to answer. Even when we want to live with courage, it's not easy to live with courage. But sometimes we have to lean our bodies out over our lives. Sometimes we have to make essential crossings from where we are to where we know God wants us to be. And sometimes we have to take a deep breath and pray and know that there is One who is with us. And sometimes we have to say to ourselves, "Now, what is it that I'm really afraid of?"

Questions for Reflection

1. Name one of the most stormy times in your life. What happened? What was it like?

2. How did you make it through the storm? Did you feel that God was helping you? How did God help you in the storm?

3. Does the expression *If you can't get out of it, get into it!* speak to your life in any meaningful way?

9

Spiritual Rules
for a New Millennium

Scripture Text—Joshua 3:7–17

The LORD said to Joshua, "This day I will begin to exalt you in the sight of all Israel, so that they may know that I will be with you as I was with Moses. You are the one who shall command the priests who bear the ark of the covenant, 'When you come to the edge of the waters of the Jordan, you shall stand still in the Jordan.'" Joshua then said to the Israelites, "Draw near and hear the words of the LORD your God." Joshua said, "By this you shall know that among you is the living God who without fail will drive out from before you the Canaanites, Hittites, Hivites, Perizzites, Girgashites, Amorites, and Jebusites: the ark of the covenant of the Lord of all the earth is going to pass before you into the Jordan. So now select twelve men from the tribes of Israel, one from each tribe. When the soles of the feet of the priests who bear the ark of the LORD, the Lord of all the earth, rest in the waters of the Jordan, the waters of the Jordan flowing from above shall be cut off; they shall stand in a single heap."

When the people set out from their tents to cross over the Jordan, the priests bearing the ark of the covenant were in front of the people. Now the Jordan overflows all its banks throughout the time of harvest. So when those who bore the ark had come to the Jordan, and the feet of the priests bearing the ark were dipped in the edge of the water, the waters flowing from above stood still, rising up in a single heap far off at Adam, the city that is beside Zarethan, while those flowing toward the sea of the Arabah, the Dead Sea, were wholly cut off. Then the people crossed over opposite Jericho. While all Israel were crossing over on dry ground, the priests who bore the ark of the covenant of the LORD *stood on dry ground in the middle of the Jordan, until the entire nation finished crossing over the Jordan.*

Biblical Reflections

This is another crossing-over story. The Bible has many of them, and well it should because God is in the business of helping people cross over. Faith is risk, adventure, the trust to move forward into life—not always sure of the result, but knowing that God is with us in all our many crossings. This idea of crossing into the promised land is a significant one in the history of Israel, and it also is significant for the church.

Don't we all have crossings of one sort or another in our lives? And isn't it true that in our times of crossing, changing, transitioning, our lives become open to the presence of God? This is why change is not bad. In fact, as Alfred North Whitehead has said, "God is participating in the creative advance of life." That's exciting!

There are some troubling places in this text. One is the violent way God moves Israel into the land, a land occupied by other people. Secondly, the supernatural quality of the story may seem troubling, too.

Rather than getting hung up on the surface details of the text such as the violent seizing of land, a concept and practice which should be rejected on moral grounds, I would suggest that the listener find the inner essence of the text. That's really true of any biblical text. The question every reader of the Bible needs to keep asking is: What is the theological essence of this text? Too many times people get snagged on the ancient details of the text, none of which is unimportant, and fail to discover the inner workings of the biblical story. This is the place where the word of God touches the human experience of the reader. Questions this text raise are: Where am I crossing over? What is my promised land? What is God calling me, or my church, or my world to do?

This story found in the book of Joshua is a story of God's calling and helping people in the process of life transition. The people of God are trying to move into a new place with a new identity. In the sermon, I take the theme of crossing over and invite the church to reflect on what it means to cross over into a new millennium. Using the language of our computer/technological age, I try to encourage people to find new energy and courage for the next century. Implicit in the reading and sermon is the profound belief that in all changes the divine being is calling us forward.

Sermon Text

This morning our scripture reading reflects one of the most dramatic moments in the history of Israel. Therefore, it's dramatic for you and me, too. Generations of waiting and longing and praying come together at this moment on the shore of the river Jordan. Remember now, for nearly 400 years Israel had been in Egyptian bondage. Oppressed. Humiliated. Ridiculed. And then after they finally crossed the Red Sea in that made-for-movie scene with Moses' parting the waters and Miriam's dancing wildly on the other side, they endured years of wilderness wanderings. They wandered, looking for the promised land of God. They wandered, looking for nothing less than home.

But at this moment, at this moment on the shore of the river, there is no more slavery. At this moment there is no more wandering. It is now time to take a step, move the body. It is now time to cross over.

Let me give you a little hint about reading the Bible. Anytime you have a scene in the Bible where there is a river, you'd better open your eyes a little wider. Rivers are symbolic of spiritual change. To go to the river is to face a moment of transition with God. It means more than simply going from this side to that side. To go to the river means that we are trying to find that place where God wants us to live. Rivers are liminal places. Those places where we live in between where we have been and where we're supposed to go. No wonder the essayist Edward Abby has written that "every person must eventually go down to the river."

What would it mean for you this morning to go down to the river of God?

I know that this story is about Joshua and the deacons carrying this little ark of the covenant across the river and over to the promised land; about how God was with them; about how their Birkenstock sandals didn't even get wet. But let's bring the story home this morning. Where does God want your spiritual life to be today? What crossing do you need to make? What spiritual potential is possible for you?

I received a letter not long ago from someone who asked me a very simple question. She wrote, *How do I get started living as a Christian?* The question is so simple, but there's really nothing simplistic about it, is there? *How do I get started?* I then read and reread this story of crossing the river Jordan from the book of Joshua, and I think I found at least a beginning answer for her. And since she works as a computer programmer, I thought I might try to download my answer into her language instead of my language this morning. Let's see how it goes.

The first insight that I need for a spiritual crossing is this: *You've got to power up!* Now that may not seem like much to you. But for those of us afraid of computers—who know, just know, that they're going to mess up our lives or make us feel dumb or just plain humiliate us—finding the courage to turn the thing on is no small task.

The spiritual life must be turned on, too! Or if you like the biblical image better, if you want to meet God, then you've got to go down to the river and cross over!

How many people, I wonder, are afraid to start going to church because they've built up in their minds that church is only for a certain kind of person, and since they've never thought of themselves as that kind of person, they just stay home? How many people have wanted to go to a Sunday school class but never do so for fear of looking or sounding or feeling dumb? How many people have wanted to try to read the Bible at home or say a daily prayer but just don't do it for fear of feeling silly? How many of us have wanted to ask deeper questions of our faith, but we don't because we're afraid we might not find the same old traditional answers? And I wonder this morning, how many of you would really like to become more involved in service to the community, but there's a little voice that says to you, "Oh, just forget it. University Christian Church doesn't need you." How many of you have heard that voice?

I want to make sure every one of you hears what I'm about to say this morning. Don't ever ignore your spiritual impulses! There is within every human being this dynamic quality of spiritual energy. Don't ignore it. In fact, my hunch is that at least some of our neuroses and depressions and even diseases are cries of the body to attend to our soul. Therefore, don't ignore your spiritual impulses to be close to God. Instead, turn on the switch and power up. Think about it. For years Israel had thought about the promised land, had talked about the promised land, had prayed about the promised land. But there comes that dramatic moment when it is time to believe that God is with you, and then you put your foot in the river. Crucial to the spiritual life is taking the first step. You've got to power up!

The second spiritual rule is this: *You've got to surf the Net!* I've not done much of it, but those of you who have been on the Internet know that there is a whole other universe out there of people and informational connections. What you immediately discover on the Internet is that there are people out there who are interested in some of the same things you're interested in. There are people who have intriguing ideas that you can utilize. And, most of all, what you find on the Internet are fascinating surprises.

Part of the spiritual adventure is surfing our life experiences in order to find our God connections. There is a presence of God in the world that flares up, that quietly whispers, that surprises us in ordinary life. Michael Murphy calls it "these incredible nearnesses."

I want to tell you about one of my incredible nearnesses. His name was Dennis. I don't even remember Dennis' last name, but what I do remember is that it was Youth Sunday. The youth were going to do it all—the music, the communion, the sermon. Youth Sundays scare senior ministers to death; you never know what they're going to do.

Dennis was thirteen years old. He had a squeaky voice and a mousy appearance to go along with it. Dennis had volunteered to sing a solo for Youth Sunday. He took his place in front of the congregation. A friend of his was playing the guitar. Dennis starting singing a song by Eric Clapton, *Tears in Heaven*. I can still see him, sitting on the stool, a little music stand in front of him. And Dennis sang the song:

> Would you know my name
> If I saw you in heaven?
> Would it be the same
> If I saw you in heaven?

As he went on and on, I could begin to feel the congregation fidget, and I started to fidget, too. I could feel myself turning red with embarrassment for Dennis, for his family, for the whole church. Not only was this song sounding awful, at the pace Dennis was going it wouldn't finish until about two in the afternoon. But Dennis kept right on singing:

> I must be strong
> And carry on,
> 'Cause I know I don't belong
> Here in heaven.

And just when I didn't think he was going to be able to finish the song, he found the courage and the breath to bring it to a completion. And when he finished there was dead silence in the sanctuary. The kids in the youth group wanted to giggle. I could tell they wanted to giggle. But even they were silent. For a moment the church didn't know what to do. It was awful, and everyone in that sanctuary that morning knew it was awful.

Then something happened. It was as if everybody recognized at the exact same time what guts it took for Dennis to sing that song. He didn't care. Why, he didn't even notice that he sounded a little foolish. He sang the song because in his own awkward, naive, adolescent way, he sang it because he loved God. That's it. That's really it. HE...LOVED...GOD.

It felt like the silence in that sanctuary lasted forever. And then someone—it must have been his mother—started to applaud. And then the entire church applauded. And then people stood up and applauded. They had never applauded for any of my sermons! And I was amazed and surprised. And I was touched by that little boy and the pure lesson of faith he had given me.

Friends, you never know where you will discover a God connection. Who would have thought that standing in the middle of the Jordan River, holding this little holy box called the ark of the covenant, would become a definitive spiritual experience for Israel? But it did. And for us, too, in strange and unusual places and sometimes through strange and unusual people like Dennis, God teaches us lessons, draws near to us with presence, guides us in providential directions. And that's why we surf the Net of our living, because sometimes in our ordinary moments something extraordinary is discovered.

My last rule for the spiritual life is this: *Reprogram your software!* Now I don't know much about computer hardware and software, but in comparison to people, this makes sense to me. There's a part of who we are that will probably never change because that's our basic human personality, our hardware. But there's another part of who we are that's up for revision and change and transformation; that's the software part of our personalities. And it's in the software of our lives that we can make decisions, take responsibility, move toward that which we value the most.

Let me tell you something about that day of crossing over for Israel. Their movement toward the promised land had to have been difficult, not because the promised land wasn't there, but because they had gotten used to the idea of Egyptian bondage, had become accustomed to wilderness.

For me at least, one of the most interesting questions Jesus would ever ask people was, "Do you want to be well?" Do you *want* to be well? And that can be translated: Do you want a healthier life? Do you want a better marriage? Do you want more positive relationships? Do you want a more meaningful walk with God? Do you want to make a bigger difference in the world? You see, the essence of the Christian life is not about the amount of information you know about God; it is about the quality of transformation you experience from God.

And that's exciting because that means you can reprogram the old grudge into the new forgiveness. You can reprogram the old grieving into the new living. You can reprogram the old apathy into the new involvement. You can reprogram the old anger into the new understanding. You can reprogram the old destructiveness into the new vitality. The apostle Paul put it like this in the book of Corinthians, "If anyone is in Christ, there is a new creation!" And new creation is what it is all about.

And so that's what I would say to my friend who wrote to me wanting to get started in her Christian life. The new millennium beckons all of us this morning to power up—getting started. And then to surf the Net—looking for the unexpected God connections. And then to reprogram the software—knowing that God is waiting for us to live the spiritual life we are destined to live. Power it! Surf it! Reprogram it! Those are the rules for spirituality as we cross into the next century—or for that matter, anytime you're ready to go down to the river.

Questions for Reflection

1. What is one "power up" step you could take for your spiritual life?

2. Name a spiritual moment in your life when you felt surprised by God.

3. What is one destructive—or less than healthy—habit that you would like to reprogram for your personal spiritual growth?

10

Living God—
So Much like a Woman

Scripture Text—Luke 18:1–8

Then Jesus told them a parable about their need to pray always and not to lose heart. He said, "In a certain city there was a judge who neither feared God nor had respect for people. In that city there was a widow who kept coming to him and saying, 'Grant me justice against my opponent.' For a while he refused; but later he said to himself, 'Though I have no fear of God and no respect for anyone, yet because this widow keeps bothering me, I will grant her justice, so that she may not wear me out by continually coming.'" And the Lord said, "Listen to what the unjust judge says. And will not God grant justice to his chosen ones who cry to him day and night? Will he delay long in helping them? I tell you, he will quickly grant justice to them. And yet, when the Son of Man comes, will he find faith on earth?"

Biblical Reflections

Occasionally parables and stories need to be turned upside down or inside out or viewed from underneath in order to find a new insight. Typically, this parable has been read identifying God as the judge. And I think it's true that God may well be like a judge. Yet, like most metaphors, it only goes so far. What I decided to do in this parable is turn it upside down and ask questions such as: Is God like the woman? Are we like the judge? What would happen if we reversed the parable?

Over the past years many scholars have asked us to see the feminine image of God. To suggest that God is actually a goddess seems to miss the point. God is beyond every image, yet in need of image if we are to experience the living presence of God. I think it's fine to address God as father. But it's also fine to address God as mother. It's also fine to think of God as brother or sister. It's fine to think of God within a vast array of images. Truthfully, the more images we use to access God, the richer our faith experience.

But more than focusing on the feminine image in this parable, I try to suggest that God uses power more in keeping with the begging woman than the aloof judge. This sermon brings into question the whole issue of theodicy—how God works and rules in the world. Those familiar with process theology will clearly see that I'm offering a theological alternative to classical theism, which has traditionally affirmed that God knows all, is all-powerful, and is all-present. Rethinking how God uses power in the world is one of the most important theological undertakings we can engage. I address this question more fully in my book *Finding a Faith That Makes Sense* (Chalice Press, 1996).

Additionally, it's important to note that Luke frequently makes women into the heroines of his stories and narratives. The role of Mary, the mother of Jesus, is significant in Luke's Gospel. In my mind, Mary becomes the quintessential image of the feminine dimension of God. Women are the first to discover and announce the resurrection, and in that sense they become the prototypical "first believers." The fact that women are portrayed so positively in the Gospel of Luke should make thinking of God in feminine terms much easier to appreciate.

Sermon Text

There was a judge. Not just any judge, but a judge who was considered hard, even calloused, a judge that had heard it all before. He didn't much care for people. Didn't much care for God. He was a judge who wore his robe as a wall between him and the people, a man who sat high above the hurts and complaints of others. He heard the pleas but never felt them; he watched the parade of people but never really saw them.

But there was also a woman, a widow. The fact that she was both widow and woman indicates that she was among society's most vulnerable. Remember now, this was in the days before Social Security and IRAs. Unlike the judge who sat above the human experience, she was right smack in the middle of it. And in that human experience, she had to fight and scrape for her dignity. She had to cry and cajole just to survive. And when someone tried to take her to court, all she could do was knock on the judge's door, knuckles bleeding, voice pleading, asking the judge to notice her. And as the story goes, the judge finally does answer her.

Not because he really cares as much as because he's worn down, exasperated, annoyed by her ceaseless persistence. The persistent widow finally receives her justice.

It's a nice little parable, isn't it? What's interesting is that after the telling of the parable we find at least one interpretation of it in the Gospel of Luke, namely, as Christians we're supposed to pray ceaselessly, never give up, and remember that what may seem like God's indifference is not indifference at all but delay.

Now, that's the parable as we find it in the Gospel of Luke. And certainly the point that we should never give up in our praying is a valid one, but that's not what I want you to focus on this morning. Instead, I want you to rethink this parable. I want you to grab hold of this parable with your imagination and turn it upside down. Because what I really want you to do this morning—and it's a big challenge I know—is to rethink your theology, your beliefs, your fundamental assumptions about God.

When most of us hear this parable, we make the quick application that God is like the judge and we are like the widow—praying, desperately needing the all-powerful, all-knowing, all-present God to help us out in life. In fact, in the Bible often the metaphors used to talk about God are metaphors like the judge, the king, the father. Those aren't the only biblical metaphors, but they are the ones we frequently seem to hear in church. And in some ways, this parable reinforces what might be called a "classical" view of God, a view that most of us probably received as children. Remember that little prayer—"God is great, God is good, now we thank him for our food." Think about it, in that one little prayer we've identified God as the Being in the world who has all the power, who is morally good, and who is male. That's a lot in one little prayer, isn't it? The classical theistic viewpoint defines God as eternal, changeless, independent, unrelated to the world—kind of like a judge. Augustine said that "God is untouched by want or change." Anselm defined God as "Supreme immutability," which means that God is beyond all passion and change. Yet, Anselm could never figure how God could be without "passion" and still be "compassionate." That's a problem with a classical view of God.

Here's the challenge this morning. Let's turn the parable upside down. What if in the parable the picture of the judge is not a picture of God, but a picture of you or me? What if the judge—cold, ruthless, resistant—is really a picture of our indifference toward others, our apathy to human suffering, our smugness to the hurting of our world?

And what if the one knocking on the door, the woman begging at the chamber door of the judge, crying and desperate for a place in the world, what if that is actually a picture of God? What if the picture of God in this parable is a picture of vulnerability? What if this unforgettable woman is really God pleading to come into a place of recognition in our lives and the lives of others?

Sometimes we see only what we'll let ourselves see. When you turn the parable upside down, what you see is that God is not like the infamous Judge Lance Ito, wielding power before a national television audience. Do you want to know what God is *really* like? God is like Fred Goldman, crying hot angry tears for a murdered son—so hurt, so full of love, so desperate that he can hardly be consoled. That's what God is like. Do you want to know what God is *really* like? Look into the eyes of Denise Brown when she makes an appearance on *Larry King Live*, and see her intensity, her desperation to recover some crumb of justice for her sister in this world. That's what God is *really* like.

I know most of us prefer the images of the emperor king or the invincible judge or the benevolent but stern father when it comes to "metaphoring" God. And all of those images shed some insight into God. In a way, God is like a king or judge or father. But these images alone cannot paint the whole picture of God. Because beyond the classical theism most of us have inherited, there is a way of understanding God—not as unrelated, but as deeply related to the world. Full of love. Full of passion. And, yes, complete with vulnerability as God invites and encourages and works to have a place in our lives. God is like a widow.

Recently I had a chance to see the movie *Shine*. It's really a marvelous movie, and in the end there is portrayed a triumph of the human spirit that I found absolutely inspiring. It's the story of a child who possesses an immense talent for playing the piano. But this little boy also has a father who is controlling, even to the point of being abusive. The boy's talent never really gets to break out and shine because his father is so closed and demanding. The movie takes you through the boy's childhood and then adolescence and then that terribly painful moment when, against his father's wishes, he breaks away from the house and goes away to school in London. But the pain and abuse of his childhood finally catch up with him, and the young man has a total emotional breakdown. Consequently, he lives much of his adult life in mental hospitals, rejected by his family, alone, unable to function in society, and, tragically, unable to use his musical genius.

But then a miracle happens. A waitress at a local cafe takes an interest in him. She begins helping him, an expression of genuine human caring. (Miracles can always happen through genuine human caring.) Through the waitress, he meets a woman. And though he is not what you might call a completely "independent, functioning adult," he nevertheless falls in love with the woman, and she falls in love with him. And it is that experience of love that finally makes his life whole. In one of the most beautiful scenes I've ever seen, this man, having been so vulnerable to the cruelty of life, is transformed by love and gives one more piano concert. After he plays the last note, the audience explodes with applause because they know they are in the presence of musical genius. The man, David Helfgott, stands on the stage, wearing a white shirt, glowing with all the stage lights, his whole life shining. It's almost a transfiguration.

Isn't it interesting that the real picture of God in that movie is not the father, though that's been our primary metaphor in the church for God? The real picture of God in the movie is the boy. The one hurt by life. The one who endures through life. The one scarred and broken by life. The one who finally waits for the right moment to shine through in life. That's God.

What is God *really* like? Could it be that God is like a widow who pleads at our door to have us pay attention to her? Could it be that God is like a sweet, vulnerable piano-playing genius who waits for the right moment to shine through in our lives?

But if a parable and a movie aren't enough for you today, let me offer you one more look at God. This time I want you to see a lowly Galilean. He lived nearly two thousand years ago. He was not wealthy but somehow lived a rich life. He was not regal, though some tried to make him a king. He touched lepers, risking leprosy himself. When those around him cried, he cried, too. When asked to judge others, he found ways to forgive. He compelled no one to be his follower, but with his words and actions he invited people to rediscover God. And when he could have defended himself from death, he was vulnerable enough to die his death.

The apostle Paul would summarize the life of Jesus by saying in the book of First Corinthians that "God's foolishness is wiser than human wisdom, and God's weakness is stronger than human strength."

Strange concept, isn't it, this concept of the weakness of God? As a little boy my definition of God was that of an invisible being who could do anything in the world. God was like a superhero—part Batman, part Spiderman, part Superman! But Jesus Christ helps me see it differently. In the story of Jesus, I see a powerful God, but God's power is the power of persuasion, of invitation, of reason, of compassion, of love. And that perhaps is the hardest thing in the world to understand about God. Yes, the Roman soldiers had a certain kind of power when they nailed his innocent body to a cross. But wasn't it more powerful when that dying Christ turned to those same soldiers and prayed, "Forgive them...they know not what they do"?

I saw a cartoon in the *New Yorker* magazine not long ago. Two decorated generals were looking up at the sky while several fighter jets flew overhead, showing off their impressive speed and skill. One general whispered to the other, "Hard to believe that there's not a military answer for everything." And it's true. What ultimately changes the world is not military power or dictator power or king power or judge power. Finally, there must be the power of invitation, the power of becoming weak, the power of loving but risking the rejection of love. That's the kind of power that changes the world.

You know what I think? I think God is knocking on the door of our lives over and over again, wanting us to pay attention, to grow in our spiritual lives. Have you ever had the feeling: "Is this all there is?" Or the feeling: "There's still something missing in my life"? Those feelings are like the widow knocking on the door of our lives. And many of us deny those feelings or try to answer them with going shopping, or eating, or going out to lunch and then shopping. Or we stay at the office a little later each day, or divorce, thinking someone else will make us happy this time. In the meantime, God still knocks on our door. Vulnerable to the point of risking our rejection but waiting on us to pay attention and develop a relationship.

We're at a new point in our family. Our kids are starting to go out and do things with friends. And that's fine. The trouble is that they now stay out longer than I can stay awake at home. I try to stay awake. But honestly, I don't know when anybody in our house goes to bed anymore. I don't even know who's in the house anymore. So now when I get up in the morning—at least I do get up before anybody else—I ask Marti, "Did the kids get home okay?" She says, "Yes." I'm always glad to hear that. One morning last weekend, I said to her, "Did you stay up until they got home?" And she said, "Of course, I stayed up. You don't think I can go to sleep unless they're home, do you?"

That's the picture. A woman at home waiting. At one and the same time strong, because there is no one stronger than their mother, and also vulnerable, vulnerable because she aches for their well-being, especially when they've gone out for the evening. It's the kind of love that can keep you up all night long. And I thought about it all weekend. Thought about it until it finally hit me. That is so much like a *woman*. So much like *God*.

Questions for Reflection

1. Do you experience the image of a vulnerable God positively or negatively?

2. Have you ever gone through a period in your life when you knew that God was "waiting up" for you?

3. Can you name an example in your life where "weakness" was actually amazing strength?

11

Where Is God when Life Doesn't Go Right?

Scripture Text—Romans 8:18–27

I consider that the sufferings of this present time are not worth comparing with the glory about to be revealed to us. For the creation waits with eager longing for the revealing of the children of God; for the creation was subjected to futility, not of its own will but by the will of the one who subjected it, in hope that the creation itself will be set free from its bondage to decay and will obtain the freedom of the glory of the children of God. We know that the whole creation has been groaning in labor pains until now; and not only the creation, but we ourselves, who have the first fruits of the Spirit, groan inwardly while we wait for adoption, the redemption of our bodies. For in hope we were saved. Now hope that is seen is not hope. For who hopes for what is seen? But if we hope for what we do not see, we wait for it with patience. Likewise the Spirit helps us in our weakness; for we do not know how to pray as we ought, but that very Spirit intercedes with sighs too deep for words. And God, who searches the heart, knows what is the mind of the Spirit, because the Spirit intercedes for the saints according to the will of God.

Biblical Reflections

This reading is one of the best known in the entire New Testament. And well it should be! It portrays in poignant fashion the enduring presence of God, even in the face of suffering and tragedy.

The issue of how God works in the world is one of the most difficult to address. Some portray God as being responsible for evil. Others suggest that God doesn't cause evil but allows it. Still others suggest that God allows evil to accomplish a greater good. All are possibilities, and I try to raise these possibilities in the sermon.

For me at least, the question of God and human suffering is *the* theological issue to be addressed. If this one cannot be addressed, then all other claims about God are muted. In a post-Holocaust world, human suffering must be addressed as never before. One penetrating question for anyone concerned about theodicy (how God rules) is: *Does what we believe about God make sense in front of the open ovens of the Holocaust?* So much for easy answers.

In the sermon, I try to take a real-life situation and address it from a theological perspective. I wish more of theology would do this. After all, it's life that we're all trying to figure out. My hope is that people will realize that it's not just a minister who has to answer the tough questions of human loss and suffering. Finally, that question comes around to every thinking Christian.

Sermon Text

I'll never forget the phone call that came to me in December 1995. It was cold outside, snow on the ground, just a few days before Christmas. We had planned as a family to go out that afternoon and buy our Christmas tree. The call came on that Saturday morning. On the other end of the line was a member of my church. Her voice was broken, filled with panic. In between the heavy sobs, I could barely make out the message: "We're at the hospital. It's Mom. We think she had a heart attack. We think she's gone."

Immediately I got in my car and headed to the hospital. As I drove, I found my mind racing: "Could it be? Not Sue, surely not Sue. She's too young. It can't be. Last week she sang a marvelous solo at church. Played the piano at our Christmas party. It can't be Sue. There was to be a Christmas party at her house this week. She loved Christmas. Literally, a Christmas tree in every room. Nobody loved Christmas like Sue. And what about her son, Chris? What's going to happen to Chris? He's only twelve years old. He's so attached to her. Our choir will be devastated. Sue was the glue that held the choir together. Music was her passion. No, there must be some mistake. Not Sue."

I pulled up to the hospital, went through the emergency room doors, turned to the right, and found the grief-stricken family. I had been with them before on so many happy occasions, but not this time. This time their eyes were red and puffy, faces white. They looked almost ghost-like. The oldest daughter, Debbie, came up to me, gave me a hug, and thanked me for coming to the hospital. The husband, Bob, just sat in one of those plastic waiting room chairs, unable to even get up and acknowledge my presence. But what I'll never forget is a twelve-year-old boy, whose cry I can still hear, sitting in a chair asking, "Why? Why? Why did this happen to my mom? Why did *God* do this to my mom?"

He didn't know it, but he was asking one of the deepest theological questions any person can ask—that question of *why*. *Why* did this happen? *Why* did God *cause* this to happen? *Why* did God *allow* this to happen? *Why? Why?*

For a few moments this morning I want to talk about that *why*. But to do that I first of all need to say that I know suffering is not theoretical. Some of you have had or do have deep human suffering, and I would never want to minimize it by trying to figure it out or explain it or use it as a mere illustration. At the same time, my faith in God—and I think your faith, too—seeks a level of understanding. Not that we can explain everything, but if faith is really faith it calls us to address the ultimate *whys* of life. The other thing I want quickly to say is that I don't assume I have all the right answers regarding God and suffering. There are brilliant theologians who have different ideas than I'm going to present to you today, and I respect them. But all I can do this morning is share with you what, to this point in my life, makes sense about this deepest *why* in human experience.

From a classical theistic point of view, people have affirmed that God is both omnipotent and benevolent. Therefore, when bad things happen—bad things like an automobile accident, a plane crash, a twelve-year-old losing his mother—when those things happen, we ask *why*. And we ask it because we assume that since God has all the power and since God is good, God could have and should have stopped it from happening. Why didn't God stop that heart attack? Why didn't God stop that plane from crashing into the Atlantic Ocean? Why didn't God stop a crazed gunman at the top of the Empire State Building last week? Isn't God good? Doesn't God care? Why didn't God intervene, just break through the thin veil of human experience and stop the bad thing from happening?

As Christians we've tried to answer the *why* question in a couple of different ways. Some have suggested, not too seriously, but suggested that maybe God *isn't* so good. Á la the psychologist Carl Jung, who developed the idea that every human being has a shadow side, maybe God has a shadow side. Does God ever go into a dark mood? Does God have a bad day and, therefore, just to release a little tension crashes a plane, starts a little cancer, causes a flood? If you remember the recently re-released

George Lucas film, *Star Wars,* you'll remember that Darth Vader is something of a God symbol, of the "dark side" of the divine. Does God have a
dark side?

Now, I've thought about that view of God as an option. But finally, at
least to me, that view of God is reprehensible. That kind of God is not
worthy of my worship, doesn't appeal to the best of who I am as a human
being. That kind of God is no better than a Unabomber causing hurt and
heartache on the basis of a whim. And so to suggest that bad things happen because God is having a bad day runs against everything that is finally
right about life.

A second option, and the one that I find a lot of Christians trying to
live with, is the idea that God has all the power and God is good, but that
God either causes or allows bad things to happen in order to accomplish
a greater good beyond our comprehension. That means that God caused
Sue to die of a heart attack, allowed this little boy now to live the rest of
his life as a motherless child, but that God really was working a greater
good out of this tragedy. From our limited perspective it may look bad,
but it's not really bad, because God is working a greater good.

But do you see the problem with that viewpoint? To say that it only
looks bad but is not really bad is to diminish the reality of the situation. I
had a chance to watch the movie *Schindler's List* recently. Did you happen
to watch it? It's a jarring film. I've been thinking about it all week. That
film reminds me that there is no way to overstate the horrors and human
suffering of the Holocaust. But do you see how diminishing it is to say
that the Holocaust only seemed to be an evil, only looked like a tragedy?
That what God really was trying to do was to create a larger good that
might come forth from the death of six million Jews? To me, such a view
of God is not only unimaginable, but unconscionable.

So how do we respond to that *why* of life? I want to suggest that there
are events in life that God doesn't cause, that God doesn't allow, but they
happen anyway. And those events are contrary to the very essence of God.
The central being of God is love, mercy, and justice. In light of that, the
Holocaust was against God's will. A child losing his mother to heart disease is against God's will. A child accidentally killed by a handgun lying
around the house is against God's will. A flood that wipes out an entire
town is against God's will. A bunch of cowards calling themselves "God's
Army" detonating a bomb in a gay nightclub in Atlanta is against God's
will. Bad things happen. No, really bad things happen. But just because
they happen doesn't mean that God has caused them or even that God
has allowed them. It just means that they have happened in a radically free
world.

Now, is it the case that good can come from bad? I think the answer is yes. I'm amazed at how some people have survived, even flourished, in the most difficult of circumstances. In fact, most of my heroes in life are people who are survivors and thrivers! And that's some of you. Because I know that some of you have endured the indignities of war or disease or financial loss or family tragedy. You've been there. You have walked the valley of the shadow of suffering. Yet, you're also here this morning. And that's testimony that you continue to believe in your ability to live life, to enjoy love, to make a contribution to others. Scarred? Yes. Defeated? No. You have become a stronger person, a better person through your suffering. But that recognition is a million miles away from saying that God caused or even permitted your tragedies.

Why then do *really* bad things happen to *really* good people? For me, what I've had to conclude is that the world is radically free. And freedom is a wonderful thing, but it is always a daring, dangerous, dizzying thing. Think about it. With your freedom you could devise a new instrument that a doctor might use to save the life of a child, and with your freedom you could devise a bomb and blow up a federal building in Oklahoma City. With your freedom you can drive a car on vacation and experience new parts of the country, and with your freedom you can get drunk, drive your car, and kill another human being. But do you see that the good in the world and the bad in the world come from the same place—that place of radical freedom? To be fully alive as a human being means that we use our freedom, but it also means that we experience the consequences of our freedom and, yes, the consequences of the freedom of other people.

Now hearing that, you may feel a little bit like that first grader I knew back in Kentucky. His grandmother told me that on the first day of school, when he had been there for half a day, he started packing up his supplies, getting ready to go home. The teacher said to the little boy, "Billy, what are you doing?" And the little boy said, "It's lunch time. It's time to go home." The teacher then tried to explain, "Well, Billy, you're in first grade now. In kindergarten you only stayed a half day, but now in first grade we eat lunch at school and stay all day." The little boy thought about it for a second and said, "Well, who in the heck signed me up for that?"

That may be exactly how we feel about freedom. Who in the heck signed us up for that? But think about it. Isn't it better to be free and susceptible to pain, than to be a robot and not feel anything? I think there's a way to read the story of Adam and Eve in the Garden of Eden, not so much as a fall from grace as a daring and inevitable attempt to reach consciousness in a free and complicated world. With our freedom we fall in love or write poems or paint masterpieces or listen to music.

With our freedom we work in soup kitchens or start foundations or build a day-care center. Living with our freedom is what it means to be a human being.

So, what should I have said to a twelve-year-old boy asking *why* in that hospital waiting room? Well, I'll tell you what I didn't say. I didn't say something like "God took her." I didn't say something like "It must be God's will." I didn't say something like "Well, don't you worry, something good will come from this." Because to have done that would have been to diminish his hurt and present God as this inexplicable controller.

Instead, all I could do was hold him and say, "Chris, I know you're hurting. God is hurting. God is hurting, too."

And to say that may not sound like much, but it says everything. Because if God is indeed love, then God is indeed the one who suffers with us in every hurt, in every loss, in every heartache. As human beings we have heart attacks and get diseases and have accidents. Sometimes that's our doing. Sometimes that's the doing of others. Sometimes it's no one's doing; it's just life in a radically free world. But in the midst of life, God is present as a fellow sufferer, urging us to be the people we can be, but hurting with us when bad things happen. And God hurts for us because God loves us. Finally, that's the greatest gift we can receive in life— that God loves us to the point of God's own pain. No wonder Paul would say in the book of Romans that "the Spirit of God prays for us even when all we can do is groan and moan and cry; the Spirit in our suffering searches the mind of God."

The theologian Dietrich Bonhoeffer, who had suffered much in a Nazi prison and would eventually be put to death by Adolf Hitler, made a little comment in a letter he wrote from prison that changed my entire life. Maybe it will change yours, too. He said, "Only a suffering God can help." And it's true. "Only a suffering God can help." At least that's all I could come up with as I held a twelve-year-old boy in my arms.

Questions for Reflection

1. How do you understand God and human suffering?

2. Have you ever had a situation that has made the theological question of God and human suffering real for you?

3. Imagine putting that twelve-year-old in front of you. What would you say to him as he asks his questions of God?

12

The Immediate, Living Experience of Christ

Scripture Text—John 1:35–42

The next day John again was standing with two of his disciples, and as he watched Jesus walk by, he exclaimed, "Look, here is the Lamb of God!" The two disciples heard him say this, and they followed Jesus. When Jesus turned and saw them following, he said to them, "What are you looking for?" They said to him, "Rabbi" (which translated means Teacher), "where are you staying?" He said to them, "Come and see." They came and saw where he was staying, and they remained with him that day. It was about four o'clock in the afternoon. One of the two who heard John speak and followed him was Andrew, Simon Peter's brother. He first found his brother Simon and said to him, "We have found the Messiah" (which is translated Anointed). He brought Simon to Jesus, who looked at him and said, "You are Simon son of John. You are to be called Cephas" (which is translated Peter).

Biblical Reflections

Portrayed in this text from the Gospel of John is a living encounter with Jesus Christ. How much of this story is actual history is hard to know. What is apparent, however, is that John is demonstrating to the early church the beauty and power of experiencing Christ. Because of this story, Andrew came to be known as the first evangelist, one who shares the good news with another.

The title of the sermon comes from Carl Jung, who spoke of an "immediate, living experience of Christ." By the way, I retell the dream of

Jung's in the sermon, but in a slightly more agreeable way, given my audience. I became intrigued in this text with how Andrew found Christ for himself. But then Simon had to experience this encounter for himself, too. It's not enough that those around us have faith. Faith finally has to become individuated. Earlier in the book I suggested that Jesus himself desired first-hand experience of God at his baptism. Clearly the paradigm in the earliest writings of the church was an experiential faith.

The more I looked at this biblical text the more I became fascinated with the idea that it is never enough to merely learn about Christ. There is a dimension of Christian faith that is only experienced. Many of us in mainline churches are afraid of experience, but we shouldn't be. An experiential faith is not an anti-intellectual faith. Faith seeks understanding, to be sure, but it also seeks personal and community authenticity. Experience of God is what it's all about. This is especially the case in the Gospel of John, where so much emphasis is placed on the presence of the Holy Spirit.

Sermon Text

When he was a young man, the Swiss psychologist Carl Jung had a dream. He dreamed of a great church cathedral. Majestic spires. A vaulted ceiling. Stained-glass windows. As in most churches, there were burning candles. Religious symbols like cross and altar, pews and pulpit all filled the sanctuary.

But suddenly in the dream the cathedral was demolished. The ceiling caved in. The walls fell to the ground. The entire place of worship was destroyed. The destruction didn't come from the outside or from the inside; rather it came from above. In the dream, the cathedral, this house of God, was destroyed by God.

Fascinating dream, isn't it?

Carl Jung reflected on that dream his entire life. The fact that he grew up the son of a prominent clergyman is of no small significance, but what he saw in the symbolism of the dream was the idea that real faith is not the same as church, not the same as tradition. The insight he gained through the dream was that what God wanted him to have was not a faith handed to him by the church. Not a secondhand faith. Instead, what he learned was that God wanted him to have a firsthand faith. A faith that Jung would later call in his memoir "the immediate, living experience of Christ."

Have you ever had what you might call a "religious experience"? One of those moments in life when you knew you were in the presence of the divine? Maybe it was a strong feeling or awareness that a numinous, luminous moment with God had taken place. A religious experience.

It's hard to know what to do with religious experience. Part of the tradition in the Christian Church (Disciples of Christ) is that we place a great deal of emphasis on the intellectual dimension of faith. And I like that emphasis. I want a faith that seeks understanding. For me, at least, a faith that is all emotion or feeling or affect is finally not enough. I want a theology that is credible and coherent in our contemporary world. I think the intellectual component of faith is especially important as we see more and more people turn to literalism or fundamentalism. Intellect is dispensable.

At the same time, there is a dimension of faith that is experiential. That is, you can read all about the faith, you can study all about the faith, you can know all the facts about the faith, but until you have a firsthand, immediate, living experience of Christ, faith is but a theory. And that's what Jung's dream pointed him toward. Jung went to church all his life. He had received all the Christian instruction that a boy could receive. In fact, his father and several uncles were clergymen. But it was only after seeing God destroy the cathedral in the dream that Jung realized that what God wanted for him was indeed this immediate, living experience of God.

I think you see the same thing in our story from John's Gospel this morning. Jesus had just been baptized. His baptism was one of those moments when Jesus had a firsthand religious experience. But then, rather than creating admiration among people—"Did you hear about the religious experience Jesus just had?"—people started moving, seeking, journeying toward their own religious experience.

One of the disciples, Andrew, follows Jesus all the way home. Listening. Learning. Andrew has his own religious encounter. But then, recognizing what he has found in Jesus, he goes and finds his brother, Simon Peter, and says to him, "Eureka! We have found it!" That's what the word "Eureka!" literally means—"we have found it." And what Andrew found is better than California gold, because the real Eureka! moment in life is when we find God as an immediate, living, and, yes, personal reality in life. Notice, Andrew can't find it for Simon Peter. He can point the way, share the news, offer the opportunity, but the living experience of Christ comes one person at a time.

One of the privileges I have as a minister is that sometimes people tell me about some of their religious experiences. Normally what I find—not always, but normally—is that people have what appears to be a very ordinary moment, but it becomes extraordinary because of their faith and openness to God.

I have a friend, a retired Methodist minister, who lost his wife tragically in a car accident several years ago. I cannot imagine how he coped with this loss, this feeling of having his life turned upside down. But he told me about a time when he was at his lowest. It was the Saturday night before Easter. He was scheduled to preach at three services the next morning, but he hardly had the energy or creativity to say a word, let alone preach a sermon.

He told me about how he went into the dark sanctuary late that night at his church. He sat there all alone. I don't know, maybe some of you know what it's like, but have you ever reached a point when you wanted to pray, but you really didn't know how to pray or what to pray for? He sat there on the first pew for a long time. In the dark he tried to pray to God the best he could. And then, he told me, "I don't know if it was the voice of God or the voice of Christ or the voice of my late wife, but I heard, I felt I heard a voice that said, 'It's okay now. You go ahead and live your life.'"

That was a religious experience. It became for him a healing moment. A turning point. I can't explain it all rationally; at the same time, there's nothing irrational about it. I think what happened is that he found on that night before Easter the real experience of Easter. He found the immediate, the living, the firsthand experience of Christ. And you can talk about it. You can think about it. You can write about it. You can preach about it. But it's not real until it enters the realm of experience.

And that can happen in a lot of ways. I was in New York City last year for a conference. Afterward Marti flew up, and we spent a couple of days doing a little sightseeing. For me sightseeing means finding good bookstores and good restaurants! What more could a person want? Two of our best friends, Ron and Leslie, told us before our trip, "There's a restaurant you must go to. It's on the Upper East Side. It's called Restaurant Daniel. Not Daniel's. Not the Daniel. Just Daniel. You'll love it."

Well, we made reservations for a Friday night dinner at 9:30 and told Ron and Leslie that's what we were doing. We looked forward to our little trip. Three things I remember about that experience.

The first thing I remember is that as soon as I walked into the restaurant I saw sitting at the first table none other than Woody Allen. I couldn't believe it. I'm thinking, "Hey, am I in New York City or what!" I was trying to be really subtle, but I'm sure I looked like some bumpkin because I kept nudging Marti and whispering, "Look. Look. Do you see who that is? That's Woody Allen!" Finally she spoke up and said, "Scott, quit punching me. I see him already." I just didn't want her to miss anything.

The second thing I remember was that when we sat down at the table and looked at the menu, I must have looked as if I had seen a ghost.

I've had some good dinners in my life, but I suddenly realized that I was now sitting in the most expensive restaurant my taste buds had ever led me to. I knew that it would take my credit card, her credit card, and all the spare change between us just to survive the evening. But we finally said, "Oh, we're in New York City. Let's splurge a little." That's splurge with a capital S!

We had an incredible meal. Yes, we had appetizers. Yes, we had soup. Yes, we had salad. Yes, we had our entree. And guess what? That's right, we had dessert, too! Well, we split one. It was one of the best times and best meals we've ever had as a couple. About halfway through the meal I think I said something really dumb like, "Do you miss the kids?" And then we both just laughed! Of course we didn't miss the kids!

But then came the moment of reckoning. We had our last sip of cappuccino. Our waiter in that thick French accent asked if we needed anything else. And then he brought to our table that little leather folder. It always looks so nice, doesn't it, that little leather folder? I picked it up. Braced myself. Alerted the paramedics. I opened the little leather folder. There was in that folder a single business card from Daniel. I picked it up, turned it over, and I read a note—*We hope you enjoyed your dinner. Love, Ron and Leslie.*

I was stunned. Overwhelmed at this sheer moment of grace. Overwhelmed that someone would be so thoughtful, so generous, so affirming of our lives. I still think about that night. It was a religious experience because in that moment, in that city where the countless thousands feel alone, invisible, insignificant, I knew that I was not alone in the universe. That love and care and friendship had come close to me. That Christ had come close to me. Yes, through the extraordinary kindness of two friends, Christ had come close to me.

And Christ wants to come close to you, too. And I don't know what it is that Christ wants to give you. Maybe courage. Maybe forgiveness. Maybe Christ wants to bring you laughter this morning. Always love. But Christ wants to come close to you in your experience of living.

You know, as mainline American Protestants, we often put the church in the very place where we really need to put our experience of Christ. Instead of being passionate people of the Spirit, many times we become prisoners of our church committees and divisions and congregational traditions. And all of those are fine as long as they help us find Christ, but they're not fine if they eclipse Christ. God forgives us when we do this year what we did last year, especially if what we're doing no longer lets the light of Christ shine as brightly as it could. And instead of finding our own faith, how many of us warm up the faith of our parents or grandparents in the microwave of our minds? Church is great! I want people to participate in church, but the job of the church is to help people find the living experience of Christ, not just to keep the organization of the church going.

And if, as mainline Protestants, we substitute the church in the place of experience, then I also would add that I think fundamentalist-type Christians try to substitute the Bible in the place of experience. My observation is that you cannot emphasize the Bible too much, but I do think you can emphasize it improperly. Just because a person knows the Bible or has the right interpretation of the Bible or can quote the Bible, doesn't guarantee that he or she has a healing, inspiring, loving relationship with Christ. Knowing the Bible and knowing Christ are two different things. Did you notice that in one of our hymns this morning we sang the words "Beyond the sacred page I seek thee Lord, my spirit pants for thee O living word"?

It's this living word that Carl Jung recognized in his cathedral dream that was of ultimate importance. Church is important. The Bible is important. But only insofar as both lead us to the experience of Christ and are never substituted for Christ.

This morning, I want to encourage you to be open to your Christ experience. Let Christ come to you through a contemplative moment as Christ came to my friend who prayed alone in that dark sanctuary. Let Christ come to you through the kindness of a friend as I found in a New York City restaurant. But also let Christ come to you at communion when you seek forgiveness. And let Christ come to you in the shining face of a child. And let Christ come to you in service as you reach out to a neighbor. And let Christ come to you when you are so desperate you can hardly find Christ at all.

Let Christ come to you. Let *Christ* come to you. Yes, let Christ come to *you*.

Questions for Reflection

1. Have you ever had what you might call a "religious experience" in your life?

2. How can we tell the difference between genuine religious experience and when a person is actually, dangerously going off the deep end?

3. I mention in the sermon a moment of deep gratitude. Can you name a moment in life when you felt most grateful?

SECTION III

Celebration

13

Listening to the Whispers of Angels

Scripture Text—Luke 1:26–38

In the sixth month the angel Gabriel was sent by God to a town in Galilee called Nazareth, to a virgin engaged to a man whose name was Joseph, of the house of David. The virgin's name was Mary. And he came to her and said, "Greetings, favored one! The Lord is with you." But she was much perplexed by his words and pondered what sort of greeting this might be. The angel said to her, "Do not be afraid, Mary, for you have found favor with God. And now, you will conceive in your womb and bear a son, and you will name him Jesus. He will be great, and will be called the Son of the Most High, and the Lord God will give to him the throne of his ancestor David. He will reign over the house of Jacob forever, and of his kingdom there will be no end." Mary said to the angel, "How can this be, since I am a virgin?" The angel said to her, "The Holy Spirit will come upon you, and the power of the Most High will overshadow you; therefore the child to be born will be holy; he will be called Son of God. And now, your relative Elizabeth in her old age has also conceived a son; and this is the sixth month for her who was said to be barren. For nothing will be impossible with God." Then Mary said, "Here am I, the servant of the Lord; let it be with me according to your word." Then the angel departed from her.

Biblical Reflections

There is hardly a scripture reading more lovely than this one from the Gospel of Luke. Luke portrays this annunciation with such tenderness and drama that as a reader I feel as if I'm being invited into a room filled with mystery and awe. This scene forever changes the way I think and feel about God, which of course is what biblical passages are designed to do.

Some, when they read a text such as this, want to immediately focus on the virgin birth of Jesus. There are some who contend that the virgin birth proves that Jesus was the Son of God. I simply want to suggest that in this context, the virgin birth is not the focus of Luke, nor did it ever have much focus in the early church. Paul, for example, never mentions it at all. And in all likelihood, Matthew and Luke mention the virgin birth, not so much to prove that Jesus was divine, but to demonstrate that he was actually human. Their point seems to be that this one who is representing God to the world is actually connected to the human experience! Moreover, Jesus is connected to the poor and lowly and downtrodden of humanity. This is part of Mary's surprise and wonder when she is blessed with the annunciation. I often tell people, "If it is important for you to believe in the literalness of Mary's virginity, then I have no problem with that. Just don't try to make the virgin birth say more or mean more than the people who wrote about it in the first place did."

One critical question when reading the Bible is *What claim does this text make about God?* Certainly this reading says much. Following Luke's emphasis, this reading suggests that God is deeply connected to the poor and humble, a slap in the face to those who thought the rich had cornered the market on divine favor. The reading suggests a feminine quality to God. This is not a "man" story. Instead, the tenderness and beauty existing between these two women surely reflects the same about God. And perhaps most importantly, this reading offers a glimpse of a revealing, annunciating, disclosing God.

It is this last suggestion around which I crafted the sermon. I try to ask the question *Where are the annunciations today?* It is not enough, contrary to Christian fundamentalists, merely to report what once happened during the times of the Bible. I'm after the living reality, the ongoing, dynamic connection of God and world. Therefore, in this sermon I invite the listener to tune up the senses, open the eyes, ready the heart; the activity of God is still present.

Sermon Text

This morning our scripture reading is about annunciation. Annunciation. When I hear the word annunciation, I obviously think of the word announcement. But annunciation is more than announcement. Annunciation is a moment in life when you feel a spiritual calling, a religious intuition, a soulful inkling. Annunciation might even be thought of as one of those moments in life when we feel our spiritual destiny begin to clarify.

In our scripture reading this morning, it is Mary who finds herself right in the middle of a moment of annunciation. I imagine Mary looking so young, so innocent, so bewildered. Her body dressed in the modest clothes of a Jewish peasant child. The long wait of pregnancy now beginning to take hold. And then tiptoeing into the room is this messenger, this angel named Gabriel. Trumpet raised, notes ready, Gabriel enters the room eager to bring an announcement.

It's hard to know, isn't it, what to do with angels? In the last couple of years angels have been hot—very, very hot. I counted no less than ten angel books on a holiday table at Barnes and Noble recently. There's a television show on CBS called *Touched by an Angel*. I notice that even John Travolta played an angel in the movie *Michael*. It seems a little strange to me because I remember when he was a "sweathog" on *Welcome Back, Kotter*, but never mind. Angels are hot right now.

Personally, I think there's something positive in our fascination with angels. I think it's a sign of our deep longings for God. A sign of our spiritual appetite for God. Sure, angels have become commercialized a bit, but the truth is we're fascinated with angels because there is a fundamental spiritual hunger we have that will not go away, nor should it go away until we have found a spiritual home for God in our lives.

And to me, that's what angels symbolize in the Bible. They symbolize the presence of God. Angels are narrative, artistic, imaginative symbols of the divine reality in the world. And, by the way, although angels get some press in the Bible, they don't get an enormous amount of attention there. Clearly, when they are present they are representing the power of the divine. But it is an angel present in this story of Mary's annunciation that engages our imagination.

I find it interesting that every year at this time I can always count on someone coming up to me and asking, "Do you *believe* in angels?"

And my answer is always the same. I say: "Well, it depends on what you *mean* by angels. If you mean by angels that there are these invisible flying creatures complete with beating wings, flowing blonde hair, long white robes, and little halos of light around their heads, if you mean that this kind of creature literally exists in the world the way a strange creature like a manatee lives in the ocean or a hummingbird lives in the sky, if that's what you mean by angels, then I would have to say no. No, I don't believe in that kind of literalization of angels." And by the way, I find that very few people, when actually pressed about their beliefs, believe in this kind of biblical literalization.

I go on and say, "But if you *mean* by angels that there are moments in life when the spiritual presence of God guides us, comforts us, protects us, if you mean by angels that there are moments in life when God gives us insight, creativity, and courage to live our lives in faithfulness to God, then yes, I believe in that kind of angelic working of God. And I'll tell you what else, I think that kind of angelic influence is all around us if we'll open our lives to experience it, and I think it's especially around us at Christmas."

As this annunciation story goes, this story with a character by the name of Gabriel who represents the presence of God, Mary is waiting in a room in Nazareth. The angel tiptoes inside the room and says to her, "Greetings, favored one! The Lord is with you."

Someone in the Bible study that I teach on Wednesday mornings asked the question, "Why? Why Mary?" It's a great question, but there is really no answer. As Luke tells the story, there is nothing particularly re-markable about Mary. There's no indication that she had stunning beauty or scintillating intellect. She never would have made some social registry, nor was she a member of any prominent family. Mary is chosen by God, and the fact that she is chosen—not rewarded, but chosen—is an insight that tells us that God's grace is at work here. In fact, the very first words that come out of the angel's mouth might be translated, "Rejoice, Mary, you have been *graced* by God."

I want to suggest to you this morning that annunciations of grace happen all the time, that angel encounters are waiting to happen to you. I want to suggest that God over and over again calls to our lives.

In his new book, *How Good Do We Have to Be?*, Rabbi Harold Kushner tells about his experience of traveling around the country, oftentimes be-ing interviewed by people who are not necessarily practicing Jews or Christians. He says that "in virtually every radio and television studio I visited, after I had spoken about the benefits of being religious, some-one—an interviewer, a producer, a cameraman—would take me aside and tell me privately that the most inspiring religious experience he or she had undergone happened not in the church sanctuary on Sunday morning, but in the church basement or a meeting of some other twelve-step program. There was something authentically religious about what happened to them there. I asked them if they could identify for me ex-actly what it was that was so helpful, and the word they kept coming up with was *acceptance*." And I believe it because one of the most powerful annunciations we ever experience is when some person, some group, some church gives us the gift of acceptance.

One of my good friends from Louisville is Jerry Miller. Last year he had an incredible Christmas experience. He received a call from his son and daughter-in-law asking if they could bring their son, his grandson, over to his house while they attended a company Christmas party. Sounds good, doesn't it? A grandfather spending a little time with his grandson during the holiday season.

They arrived at his house and went in. The parents stood inside the doorway for a few minutes. Not long afterward, however, they walked back to the car, holding hands with the little boy, deciding to skip the Christmas party. The daughter-in-law made up some lame excuse about suddenly not feeling well. That night Jerry's son went home and scribbled a terse note to his father. I saw the note. It read:

> Dear Dad:
> I was afraid to leave my son with you tonight. I could tell you
> had been drinking again. Dad, it's time to get help.

The very next day, a Saturday morning, Jerry found himself in a place where he had never imagined himself being—in the basement of a Methodist church, confessing his own powerlessness, talking about his desperate need of grace. And what he found in that AA meeting was neither disdain nor disgust. He found acceptance—the amazing, deeply religious, highly angelic grace of acceptance. And when it happens, it is like an annunciation from God.

Someone has said that "religion is for people who are afraid of going to hell; spirituality is for people who have already been there." And I think it's true.

Jerry would be the first to confess to you that many angels have been part of his life this past year. The angel of his son who had the courage to confront his father. The angel of his grandson he wanted to love. The angel of a group of people who gave him the gift of acceptance.

I received a Christmas card this week, and inside the card was a scribbled message that read: "Please celebrate with me the first year anniversary of the rest of my life—365 days sober. Merry Christmas. Jerry."

The psychologist James Hillman argues in his new book, *The Soul's Code*, that every person has a certain call, a certain annunciation that moves us through life. Not fate really, but an acorn-like destiny that calls us to grow and live and find meaning in our lives.

I like that idea because it reminds me that my life is not a mere accident nor are my experiences in life mere chance. It also reminds me that annunciation and calling aren't something that only happen to ministers. God is in the process each and every day of calling us to the gift of acceptance and the challenge of living. Think about it like this: Just like an organist who accompanies a soloist, so God accompanies us from birth to death to life beyond death.

The Christmas story filled with stars and shepherds and angels reminds us that God is forever coming to us, gracing our lives, interrupting our plans, surprising us with opportunities. God is forever coming to us, helping us pick up the pieces of our lives, renewing our confidence for living, healing our imperfections. It's God's grace. And we make a great mistake both theologically and hermeneutically if we think of angels only in an ancient, literalistic fashion. We miss the ongoing presence of God in our lives.

I read a little line a few years ago in one of the prayer journals of Father Andrew Greeley, and I've never forgotten it. He said, "We need to *seize* all the moments of grace that we possibly can." Grace is a gift, but when we find a moment of grace, let's seize it with passion and gratitude and joy! You all know too well that grace doesn't eliminate the bad things that have happened or will happen to you. At the same time, the bad things that have happened or will happen finally cannot eliminate grace.

After Gabriel whispers his word of acceptance, Mary makes two responses to God. The first one is marvelous. Luke says that Mary "was perplexed and pondered." I like that because it helps me see that part of faith is learning how to live life in the face of God's mystery. Folks, faith doesn't mean that we have to have it all figured out. It doesn't mean that religion gives us all the answers. We diminish the Bible, and we insult the essence of faith, when we turn Christianity into some kind of "answer-book" approach to life. I think Hallmark should come out with a Christmas card that reads something like—*Wishing you a baffling, perplexing, and wondrously complex Christmas!* Because as we contemplate the miracle of God's becoming flesh in Jesus Christ, if that doesn't take our breath away and perplex us a little, we probably haven't heard the message.

But also notice that Luke portrays a second response, namely Mary's willingness to serve God in any way possible. Do you ever think about that for your life, that question about what God wants you to do? I don't know, maybe that's just minister talk, but do you ever ask yourself how you might serve God in this world? How you might be able to serve your church? How you might be able to make a contribution to the well-being of the world? God wants to work through every one of us. And that's what Mary learned that night from the whispers of an angel. God says, "I am with you." And Mary, like you and me, was asked to respond, "And, yes, God, I am with you, too."

Could it be that this Christmas there is some presence of God that comes close to you, closer to you than your own breath, closer than your own heartbeat, closer than your own fingernails? And God speaks your name. Yes, your name. And the word given to you—not a literal word, but a word nevertheless—is the word grace? Could it be that there are many annunciations whispered in this world? Many moments when in the quietness of our lives we are surprised by grace? It must be. It must be so.

Questions for Reflection

1. What are the many emotions Mary might have felt after receiving this news from God?

2. Have you ever had an "annunciation experience," a moment when you felt your life touched by divine grace?

3. Why don't we experience more grace in the world? What is it that closes our hearts, hardens our hearts, numbs our senses?

14

Investing in the
Power of People

Scripture Text—Philippians 4:1–7

Therefore, my brothers and sisters, whom I love and long for, my joy and crown, stand firm in the Lord in this way, my beloved.

I urge Euodia and I urge Syntyche to be of the same mind in the Lord. Yes, and I ask you also, my loyal companion, help these women, for they have struggled beside me in the work of the gospel, together with Clement and the rest of my co-workers, whose names are in the book of life.

Rejoice in the Lord always; again I will say, Rejoice. Let your gentleness be known to everyone. The Lord is near. Do not worry about anything, but in everything by prayer and supplication with thanksgiving let your requests be made known to God. And the peace of God, which surpasses all understanding, will guard your hearts and your minds in Christ Jesus.

Biblical Reflections

I like this reading precisely because it doesn't try to say or do too much. It's rather quiet, really. Understated. It opens up like a flower rather than hitting you over the head with a hammer. And what I especially like about it is the human touch felt in this reading.

Typically, Paul has personal greetings at the beginning and end of the letters he sent to churches, and that is true here in Philippians. He mentions names. Real people who had been partners with him throughout his ministry.

Dr. Granville Walker, longtime senior minister at University Christian Church, said in his closing sermon, "No man stands alone." That was Dr. Walker's way of concluding a ministry and acknowledging that throughout his many years at the church he had benefitted from partners, competent and caring lay leaders who worked by his side throughout his ministry. Paul is really doing the same in this reading. No minister stands alone in the great task of ministry, and any minister who does not have the capacity to acknowledge such is tragically flawed.

In the following sermon, I invite people to think about how they do and don't invest in people. It's crucial for the well-being of any church. Moreover, it is crucial for every corner of society. If we don't learn how to invest in others, there really is no society. One of the most remarkable moments in life happens when one human being believes in another. I look back on my own life and can recall person after person who had confidence in me, expected more from me, and often believed in me when I could not find the strength to believe in myself. Surely the presence of God flows through such moments and people.

Sermon Text

I don't know why, but the endings of Paul's letters have intrigued me most. I think it's because at the end of the correspondence I experience his human side, his personal side. And I love the personal dimension. It's one thing to see the performance, but it's another to have a backstage pass, shake hands with the actor, talk personally with the star. I remember in college that the lectures I liked the most were the ones when the professor would leave his or her notes and speak straight to us, let a little passion out, give a glimpse of why the topic really mattered. It's the human touch.

In our reading this morning from the book of Philippians, we get the human touch of Paul. Here he is no longer making a complex theological argument. No more soaring into philosophical heights. Instead, the language comes down to people, an utter affirmation and celebration of people.

He says, "You are my brothers and sisters."

He says, "I long for you."

He says, "You are my joy and crown."

He says, "You are my beloved."

Do you *feel* it? Forget ecclesiology for a moment. Put aside organizational theory and sociological analysis, too. That's important, but here Paul feels this human, this personal, this relational connection with the church. And they feel it toward him, too. The human touch flows in two directions. Church, finally, at the end of all correspondence, is not some abstract idea, but a network of relationships, a wondrous web of people, a delicate bouquet of lives.

We hunger for it, don't we, this personal touch in our lives? In the 1980s the sitcom that captured it best was *Cheers*. Remember the song? *Making your way / in the world today / takes everything you got / gettin' away from all your troubles / sure can mean a lot / sometimes you want to go / where everybody knows your name.* And why? It's because we have this longing to be connected with other human beings. To know and be known. To love and be loved. To touch and be touched. Belonging. Community. Relationships. This is what we hunger for as human beings.

It's probably why one of the hottest sitcoms in the 1990s is *Friends.* Now you may like it or not like it, but the show is really a running drama about what it means to invest, detach, and invest again in relationships. And no matter how maddening or funny or heartbreaking the relationships become, there is still this longing for the personal touch. Some of our college students gather as friends to watch *Friends*!

You see, the reason why I think Paul always came around to the personal importance of relationships is that he understood that the mystery of the divine is experienced when we dare look into the eyes of another human being. Isn't it interesting that sometimes in the Bible the expression "the beloved" is sometimes Christ and at other times the church? And the insight is that when I invest my soul energy in others I open my soul to the presence of Christ. That's the spirituality of relationships.

Robert Fulghum tells about one of the most spiritual moments in his life. It didn't happen in a beautiful church. Instead, it happened between two human beings.

During the year that his book *All I Really Need to Know I Learned in Kindergarten* became a best-seller he received a telephone call:

"Are you Robert Fulghum?" the woman asked.

"Yes."

"Did you place a child for adoption in 1958?"

"Yes."

"I think," she said, "that I'm your daughter."

The next week this young woman came to Seattle to meet him. He doesn't say too much about her. She is married. Has a family. Is a teacher at a university. Can you imagine the personal bridges each of them had to build just to begin talking to each other? They told stories. Shared experiences. They started investing in each other.

Fulghum writes that at the end of the visit they really didn't know what to say. Neither of them wanted to say goodbye, but they both had to resume their normal lives. Yet, sometimes silence says it all. Before she left she picked up a blank piece of typing paper from his desk, placed his hand upon the paper, and then with a pen drew around his hand and fingers. And without a spoken word, she gave him the pen, and then he traced the outline of her hand upon the outline of his own. They each put their initials on the piece of paper. Smiled. Laughed. Cried. And then she was gone.

Think of the number of people in your life this morning whose outline has been traced over your own. A loving mother. A supportive dad. A professor who took an interest in you. A mentor in business. Think of the friends whose very presence has become for you a kind of chalice from which you have tasted the love of God. No wonder Paul finally came around to his relationships with people, because in them we find the presence of the divine.

So, I wonder this morning, what would it mean for you to begin investing in people—not stocks and bonds and financial portfolios—but that human portfolio of relationships? Let me offer a couple of practical suggestions this morning.

First of all, *you invest in people by giving them the genuine gift of your listening.* There is no gift that touches us more deeply than when somebody really hears us. Stephen Covey suggests that one of the habits of an effective person is that they "seek first to understand, and only then to be understood." The biblical writer James puts it like this, "Be quick to listen, slow to speak" (1:19).

I was on a plane a few months ago, and I found myself sitting beside a young woman probably in her early thirties. Now, you need to understand that when I fly I don't really like to talk to people all that much. I figure, I'm never going to see these people again, and besides, I just want to sit here and read for a couple of hours, maybe even take a little nap. My wife isn't like that. When she flies, by the time she's landed, she's made friends with half the passengers. But for me, I guess, I just like to travel to myself.

Well, about ten minutes into the flight I looked up from my morning paper, and this woman said, "How are you doing this morning?"

"Fine. Just fine," I answered. I'm polite. I'm always polite.

She said, "Where are you going?"

I said, "Oh, I've got a little meeting to go to in Fort Worth today." (It was really my interview at University Christian Church, but I just didn't want to tell her the whole story.) But her curiosity would not be turned away.

"What do you do for a living?" she asked.

That's a *dangerous* question when you're a minister.

What happens is that some people begin immediately treating me differently when they find out I'm a minister. It's like seeing a police car on the interstate; everybody hits the brakes and slows down. And the trouble is that I start feeling self-conscious when that happens, because I would prefer that people relax and treat me like a normal person. You don't know how tempting it is on a plane to say to someone, "Oh, I'm a nuclear physicist. And what do you do?"

But the other thing that happens when people learn I'm a minister is that they want to tell me their life story. The whole story! And normally I like that, but not on planes, and especially not when I'm going to interview at University Christian Church.

But this woman wanted to talk. She was from Shepherdsville, Kentucky. Oldest daughter of eight children. She has an uncle who is a Pentecostal minister. She thought I should get to know him sometime. And did you know that she had just broken up with her boyfriend? Well, she told me about it. In fact, she told me more about her boyfriend than I ever wanted to know. For two hours this woman talked and talked and talked. And about every ten minutes she would say, "I can't believe I'm telling you all of this. I'm normally a very shy person. I just can't believe it." And for a while I was thinking to myself, "I can't believe it either."

I don't know when it happened, but something changed in the course of that conversation. I surrendered to the fact that I was not going to be able to finish reading my morning paper. And the two books in my briefcase were going to have to wait. I don't know how it happened or when it happened, but it finally dawned on me: Here was a human being who needed the gift of listening. And so I listened. In fact, I started to enjoy listening to her. The truth is that her life was a lot more interesting than mine! And although I will never see her again, for whatever reason I cannot explain, God gave me the chance to give her this human touch of listening.

Parents, do you want to invest in your children? Listen to them. Do you want to invest in your marriage? Listen to your spouse. Do you want to make a Christian witness in your department at work? Give the gift of listening to the people who work for you. Do you want to make a difference in the life of an older adult? Sit down for fifteen minutes and listen. We invest in the power of people when we offer the gift of listening.

The second suggestion is really so simple. *You invest in people when you give them a genuine word of affirmation.* Just as there is probably someone in your life waiting for you to listen, there is probably someone in your life just waiting for you to say some positive word, some affirming word, some supportive word. I'm not talking about some disingenuous compliment. I'm talking about finding ways to offer genuine affirmation to people.

I feel certain that when Paul offered his personal word to the Philippian church, he was offering a part of himself to them. And he would give himself to other people because he lived with a profound belief that God had given God's very self to him. And we can do the same. When's the last time you complimented the waitress at the restaurant? Thanked the check-out lady at the grocery? It's Parents Weekend at TCU today—I'd better say it. Students, when's the last time you told your parents how much you appreciate what they do for you? Is there an old teacher you need to write? An old friend you need to call? Is there some young man or young woman who is just waiting for your approval?

Sometimes we need to get our heads out of our own problems. Sometimes we need to move past our own moods. The interactions and potentials we have with others is tremendous. In fact, to let one day go by without moving toward another human being with support and affirmation is a shame. Folks, we need each other. And the miracle of the church is that we offer to one another the gift of our humanity, but then we move beyond the circle of the church to offer the human touch to others wherever we might find the opportunity. It's the right word at the right time that makes all the right difference.

Paul understood that the personal gift of our listening and the personal gift of our affirming are finally at the heart of what it means to be church. People matter. People matter more than committees. People matter more than schedules. People matter. When we share the gift of relationship, it is like taking our hand and tracing it over the hand of another human being. Which of course is what God did in the person of Jesus—taking God's very life and tracing it around your hurts and my wounds and our hopes. How can we do any less for one another?

Questions for Reflection

1. Name someone who has really invested in your success as a person.

2. What do you think are the characteristics of a good listener? What could you do to become more effective in your listening to others?

3. Make one commitment to offer an affirmation to another human being this week. Who is it, and what do you want to tell him or her?

15

Living in the
Now and Wow of Easter!

Scripture Text—Mark 16:1–8

When the sabbath was over, Mary Magdalene, and Mary the mother of James, and Salome bought spices, so that they might go and anoint him. And very early on the first day of the week, when the sun had risen, they went to the tomb. They had been saying to one another, "Who will roll away the stone for us from the entrance to the tomb?" When they looked up, they saw that the stone, which was very large, had already been rolled back. As they entered the tomb, they saw a young man, dressed in a white robe, sitting on the right side; and they were alarmed. But he said to them, "Do not be alarmed; you are looking for Jesus of Nazareth, who was crucified. He has been raised; he is not here. Look, there is the place they laid him. But go, tell his disciples and Peter that he is going ahead of you to Galilee; there you will see him, just as he told you." So they went out and fled from the tomb, for terror and amazement had seized them; and they said nothing to anyone, for they were afraid.

Biblical Reflections

This reading is fascinating because of the ending. Ah, another ending story. A variety of endings have been suggested for Mark's Gospel, but most scholars now agree that Mark ended his story abruptly at verse eight. It's a non-ending ending. But that's the literary genius of the entire episode. Mark leaves the ending open so that the reader is drawn in, invited to experience and participate in the resurrection. Unlike some authors who tell the whole story, Mark tells the story, but not completely, believing that the story is never completely told until it is personally experienced.

What I try to do in the sermon is invite the listener inside the sermon, to experience the resurrecting presence of Christ through words and story. It's not easy on Easter. Everyone thinks he or she knows what is coming. And in a sense they do. But God help us if we lose sight of the wonder and surprise of the Easter story. Part of the challenge in all our lives is to name places in the world where the resurrecting presence of Jesus Christ is being lived and experienced. To open our eyes each day and say, "There, that's one. That's a sign of resurrection!" is one of the gifts and challenges of Christian living.

Sermon Text

I listen to this Easter story from the Gospel of Mark, a story most of us have heard again and again and again. But rather than feeling like a "Nick at Nite" rerun, the story feels fresh, exciting, daring. The very beginning of the story signals transformation. The Sabbath is ending. Sunday morning is beginning. Light from the morning sun begins to dance off the buildings in the capital city of Jerusalem. And making their way through the narrow streets, moving toward the outskirts of the city are three women, Mary, Mary Magdalene, and Salome. Robes flowing, sandals kicking up dust, they move quietly toward the tomb of Jesus. And they go carrying jars of oils and spices, not expecting any "wow" of resurrection, but fully expecting to finish the ritual of burial.

It must have been incredibly difficult for them to live in the present moment "now" of that day. On the one hand, they could remember the good times with Jesus. Sharing a meal with him. Listening to him teach. Remembering times when he healed a leper or held a child. On the other hand, the past of bad times had to have tugged at their robes, too, as they traveled that morning. The wishy-washy Pilate. The maddening crowd. The trumped-up accusations. Before they really knew what was happening, Roman soldiers had nailed him to a cross. What could they do? What could they say? Alas, all they could do was wait and watch, wait and watch.

We all struggle with it, don't we, this challenge of living in the present moment? For many of us when we wake up in the morning, it's clear that our past has become our CEO, somehow directing our lives and convincing us that life will never be quite as happy, quite as good, quite as meaningful as it once was. Rather than living in the "now" of the present moment, we many times live in the "no" of nostalgia. And although a certain amount of whimsy and nostalgia is good, perhaps even healthy, it's not good if we find ourselves thinking, "If I could just turn back the clock, if I could just move back home, if I could just replace my loss, if I could just recreate the old situation...." That kind of nostalgia says "no" to the very gift of daily life that God offers us.

And if it's not the good times of nostalgia calling us back, many times we find ourselves wrestling with the agonizing pain of the past—pain that locks us up, cages us in, chains us down. Have you ever noticed how some people can have a failure, and that one failure defines who they are for the rest of their lives, whereas others have an equal failure, yet they somehow go on to find success? Or have you noticed how some people have a relationship come to an end, yet they grow from it, continue relating and loving others, while other people allow that one ending to block all of their loving for the rest of their lives?

I wonder this morning how many of us are leading a life like a boat in dry dock? Have you ever seen a boat in dry dock? When it's in the water the boat looks great as it motors across the lake or sails across the bay, but take it out of the water and what you see is a hull that has accumulated algae and weeds and barnacles. The trouble with all that accumulation is that it eventually creates a drag of resistance that slows the boat down.

How many of us here on this Easter morning are feeling that kind of drag of resistance in our lives? Anybody here brooding over a past mistake? Anyone here this morning carrying a grudge? Anyone sulking over circumstances totally beyond your control? Anybody here this morning still hurt or disappointed or bitter over something that happened in this church five, ten, twenty years ago? Now, we may choose to sail with all that accumulated past, but we don't have to. We don't have to because the gift of Easter is God's invitation to live in the living "now" of life!

And that's exactly what these three remarkable women discovered on that first Easter. They go to the tomb. Peek inside. They hear the announcement—"He is not here. He is risen!" The point being that if Jesus is no longer living in the past, why should you and I live in the past? If the risen Lord has courage enough to live in the "now," then why shouldn't we?

Part of what happens in the experience of Easter is that God gives us what we need to live in the grammar of present tense, not controlled by the past nor leapfrogging into the future, but living in the "now." If you need forgiveness for something in the past, God offers you forgiveness. If you need inner strength to get through a painful memory, God gives you inner strength. If you need love, God loves you to the point of God's own suffering. If you need confidence for the daily challenges of work, God believes in you and gives you confidence. I know, trust me, I know how attractive going back seems. But if Easter Sunday is to make a difference in a lifetime of Mondays, then we've got to find a way to accept God's gift of living in the "now."

But to live in the "now" means we've got to find a "wow." And the "wow" of Easter is not so much that there is life *beyond death*, though I think that's part of it. Easter, it seems to me, is more an affirmation that there is life in the *midst of death*. In daily life, in moment-by-moment living, that's where the resurrection of Christ is experienced. Yet, how many of us find ways again and again to deflect God's offer of joy?

We're not unlike that couple who went out to a restaurant and, because they had to wait for a table, found themselves sitting in a cocktail lounge. The waitress came over to them, bright and cheery, and said, "Welcome to Happy Hour. May I get you something?" The couple shook their heads and said, "No, thank you. We're just waiting on our table." A few minutes later, the waitress came back again and asked, "We sure have a great Happy Hour. May I get you a little something?" Again, they deflected the offer. "No. No, thank you. We're just waiting on our table." About ten more minutes passed and she tried one more time. "It's still Happy Hour. May I…" But before she could even finish the sentence the man said, "Look, lady, we go to church every Sunday. We're Christians. And this is as happy as we get. Just find us a table!"

Well, I've met a few Christians who live their entire life with the attitude "This is as happy as we get," haven't you? You see, part of the challenge of Easter is opening our eyes to the activity of God and receiving God's razzmatazz offer of joy in the world.

I recently read a poem by Robert Bly entitled "Things to Think." It's found in his new book, *Morning Poems*, and it is a wonderful encouragement to enlarge our expectations toward life. What I like about this poem is that it reminds us there is a mysterious "wow" trying to reach us in the "now" of our living. He uses the image of a moose rising out of the water (Is it a fascinating reference to resurrection?) and brings on its antlers a child, and that child may well be the neglected soul of our lives. He uses the image of someone knocking on our door, ready to give us something big and large and wonderful. Let's face it, sometimes we ask too little from life! Easter announces an activity of God, God's largesse, God's abundance, God's grace, and all of it is trying to break through to our human experience.

I thought about God's activity this week when I saw the cover of the *New York Times* magazine complete with a full-color portrait of Nelson Mandela. Now the leader of the new South Africa, it was not many years ago that Mandela was in prison, working eight hours a day in a rock quarry. Apartheid has been dismantled. The prisoner has become president. Justice is beginning to prevail. But do you see that those events are signs of the resurrection, of God's "wow" in this world?

This past week nearly two hundred members of the Christian Church (Disciples of Christ) gathered in Arkansas. This was no bureaucratic church meeting. From all over the country, Disciples gave up their spring break so they could help rebuild a burned church. What moved them to be there is the very same "wow" that filled those women at the tomb of Jesus two thousand years ago. It's the life-giving, joyful, Easter presence!

This past Sunday night around midnight, a group of bleary-eyed members from University Christian Church arrived back home after a week-long mission trip to Honduras. There, in one of the most remote regions of the world, they brought both help and hope. Since their return I've heard three reflections repeated by the group. The first one is the utter amazement that people in Honduras can be so poor yet so happy. The second reflection is that as soon as they got home they started planning how they could go back and do even more next time. How's that for a "wow" of optimism? The third story is that while they were at a little outdoor market, they saw used clothing for sale, and one of the items happened to be a pair of used boxer shorts, complete with the TCU logo and horned frog! Do you see that their outreach of heart and hand is a sign of the resurrecting presence of Jesus Christ in this world? Isn't that a "wow"?

And personally, I need to say today that I've been transformed by another "wow" this week. As most of you know, our community was touched by one of the deepest losses we can know with the death of a child while she was on spring break. Many of you know the family, and if you don't know them, you at least have been feeling for them. Several of our members were with them in Colorado when it happened. I spent Monday morning at Tanglewood Elementary School talking with children. I must have talked to fifty children in a three-hour period of time. They came in, one at a time, two at a time, sometimes groups of eight or ten children. And what I saw in those children utterly amazed me. They demonstrated such incredible sensitivity and compassion and insight. Those children demonstrated a capacity to feel, to grieve, to release a flood of human spirit that I'm not sure I've ever quite seen before in my entire life. It was for me a remarkable "wow" of life.

That's what Easter does, you know. Easter unleashes the flow of spirit. You can call it the Holy Spirit. You can call it the human spirit. But what you call it doesn't really matter, because it all comes from God. Easter is a "wow" because it has a way of unlocking my caged heart. It has a way of thawing that cold, growing glacier inside your soul. It's a "wow" that happens again and again and again.

Did you notice this morning how our reading from Mark's Gospel ended? It's rather strange. Mark's story ends by saying: "So they went out and fled from the tomb, for terror and amazement had seized them; and they said nothing to anyone, for they were afraid." And that's it. The story takes us to the very precipice of the mountain and then leaves us there. Sort of like saying: Here's the story of the first Easter. Now, you decide. Will you find courage to live in God's "now"? Will you open your heart to experience God's "wow"?

And Mark leaves the answer hanging because he knows that the women must find their answer and the other disciples must find their own answer, too. Will you live in the "now" and "wow" of Easter? Well, *will* you?

Questions for Reflection

1. Name a moment of resurrection, God's flow of new life, that you have witnessed or read about recently.

2. How might you lead a life more filled with the resurrection?

3. How could you share the story of good news with others in today's world?

16

Finding Heaven
when You're Mad as Hell

Scripture Text—Ephesians 4:25–32

So then, putting away falsehood, let all of us speak the truth to our neighbors, for we are members of one another. Be angry but do not sin; do not let the sun go down on your anger, and do not make room for the devil. Thieves must give up stealing; rather let them labor and work honestly with their own hands, so as to have something to share with the needy. Let no evil talk come out of your mouths, but only what is useful for building up, as there is need, so that your words may give grace to those who hear. And do not grieve the Holy Spirit of God, with which you were marked with a seal for the day of redemption. Put away from you all bitterness and wrath and anger and wrangling and slander, together with all malice, and be kind to one another, tenderhearted, forgiving one another, as God in Christ has forgiven you. Therefore be imitators of God, as beloved children, and live in love, as Christ loved us and gave himself up for us, a fragrant offering and sacrifice to God.

Biblical Reflections

This is one of those practical readings found in the literature of the New Testament. I'm aware that some have suggested that Paul didn't actually write this letter. This shouldn't be alarming, given the fact that it was common to have literature produced from a school of followers that surrounded great thinkers. The question of the authorship of this letter doesn't concern me as much as does the meaning of the words found in it.

Practically, this reading invites the reader to focus on daily matters of Christian living. Christology is important, but our Christology should make a difference in how we live daily life. How we treat one another. The attitudes we carry to work. The behaviors we exhibit at home. This is the focus of our reading.

What I do in the sermon is pick up on one of the practical themes mentioned in this reading, namely, anger. Anger is a legitimate feeling. Contrary to what some have suggested, Christians can, should, and do become angry. The question becomes what we will do with our anger after it happens. This is especially important in churches. Most churches don't know how to handle anger. It is natural within any community of faith to experience anger, and as a minister I have been both the target of congregational anger or the mediator of it. And privately, I've had a little anger of my own I've had to sort through! Unfortunately, what happens in many churches is that people simply get mad and quit. But quitting is counterproductive to what it means to be a community of faith. I relate anger to the Holy Spirit in the sermon, suggesting that to act out anger in a negative way does indeed grieve the Holy Spirit.

Sermon Text

We've all been there, driving down the road, minding our own business. You look in the rearview mirror, and there's a car right on your bumper. The driver hits the horn wanting you to speed up—or at least get out of the way. But there's really nowhere to go. He hits the horn one more time. You look in the rearview mirror again, and you see his lips are moving. It looks like he's screaming at somebody, but there's no one else in the car. He must be angry with you. You haven't really done anything wrong, but you can feel his temper exploding behind your back. You keep driving. You're going the speed limit, but that doesn't seem to be good enough. A second later he darts into the left lane, passes, then pulls right in front of you. As he speeds away, he raises his right hand in the air. For a moment, you think he might be waving good-bye. But it's not good-bye. He gives you a signal all right, but it's a signal of anger.

Anger. Powerful isn't it, this feeling of anger? I won't ask which motorist best describes you this morning, because my guess is we've been both in one way or another. Think about it this morning. Can you remember a time when someone was utterly angry with you? I bet you can. Because when someone is really angry with us, it's like a bomb exploding inside our gut, and we don't often forget it. Or can you remember when you were the bomb going off? Exploding with words you don't normally use, accusations you don't normally make, feelings you don't normally express. And although you may not enact it with physical violence, you know at least that you felt a kind of soulful violence. That's anger. Anger is like hell because hell is the ultimate symbol of a disconnect from God, from others, from ourselves. When we're raging in an angry storm, that's what it often feels like. It feels like hell.

If we're going to get anywhere this morning, we probably need to come clean and say that the church has never done very well with anger. Many churches are in denial about anger or are so scared by anger that they keep stuffing it down year after year after year. Obviously the vision of God for this world is peace. That means peace between countries, but it also means peace between people, even inner peace. Anger is so powerful and can be so damaging to others that much of the Bible encourages people *not* to be angry. And we need to hear that. Especially in our culture today where there seems to be so much unresolved grief and anger, if not rage. If you want to hear anger, just watch the talk shows for a few days. There's a lot of anger out there!

But there's another part of the Bible's message. And it's that anger is part of the human experience. Yes, that it is deeply human to be angry. And the key is not to deny the human anger that we feel but to learn how to live with it and express it in a constructive way.

Notice in our reading today that Paul first says in verse 25 that "we are members of one another." That's his way of saying that in the church, or in our families, we are in relationship with one another. Authentic relationships precede everything Paul says about behavior.

But then he also notes with striking realism that when you get people together there is bound to be some anger. If you have people, you have hurt. If you have people, you have anger. That's life. Yet, his point is not "don't get angry." He assumes that people will get angry. And, in fact, if relationships are filled with trust and love, that gives us a certain freedom to have our anger. My son can get angry at me because he knows that I will never leave him. I can get angry with my closest friends because I trust that we will work through the anger. And so, it's all right to be angry.

But what Paul does insist on is that people express their anger in a way that is finally healthy. And so, just as my doctor tells me there is "good" cholesterol and "bad" cholesterol, there is "good" anger and "bad" anger.

This morning I want to give you a crash course in good anger, so that you might find a little bit of heaven when you're mad as hell. Three words....

The first word is *acknowledgment*. If you're angry, acknowledge it. It sounds so simple, doesn't it? If you're angry with someone, go and tell that person. That's exactly what Jesus expected people to do. He said, "If a brother or sister has offended you, go and tell them." Not somebody else. Not somebody in the parking lot after the board meeting. Go and tell the person.

Yet, most of us don't tell. And sometimes we don't tell because we refuse to acknowledge even to ourselves what we're really feeling. I see families all the time that are grieving and hurting and angry, but no one will acknowledge it. It's like there's a code of silence. All the feelings have been stuffed away in boxes and hidden in the basement. Paul said, "Be angry." Be present with your feelings. Be honest with your feelings. Acknowledge your feelings.

Most of us, frankly, take the Dirty Harry approach to our angry feelings. We come home at the end of the day. We're angry at work. Angry at the boss. Angry at the quarterly numbers. We barely grunt at the kids. Don't even speak to our spouse. And then there's this little voice in the household that announces, "Let the guessing games begin!"

And we want people to guess what's wrong with us. In fact, we expect it. But as they try to guess our feelings, we give them that Dirty Harry look that says, "Well, do you feel lucky? Well, do you, punk?" The kids wonder if they've done something wrong. Our spouse wonders if he or she has done something wrong. Even the dog looks like he feels a little responsible. It's the guessing game. And instead of just honestly acknowledging that we're hurt or angry or upset, we expect people to do the impossible, namely, to read our minds. And to make it even worse we begin thinking, "If you really cared for me, you would know what's bothering me."

Do you have any idea how much better life would be if we could just acknowledge our hurt, our grief, our anger? Paul said, "Be angry but do not sin; do not let the sun go down on your anger." Which is really a very poetic way of saying that if we're angry, it's important that we acknowledge and express it.

But that brings me to my second word, and it is *responsibility*. It's crucial to take responsibility for the anger we're feeling. Two weeks ago I was trying to put some leftovers in a Tupperware container. I opened the kitchen cabinet to find some Tupperware. Well, in our kitchen cabinet it looked as if there were about four hundred Tupperware lids. And it looked as if there were about four hundred Tupperware containers. I've got to tell you that not one of those lids would fit on any of those containers. And I got angry. Just a simple lid and container, that's all I wanted.

Well, I raised my voice a little bit and said to Marti, "Why don't you organize the kitchen? You can't find anything in these cabinets!" And then, do you know what she said? She had the nerve to say, "Scott, why don't you let me help you?" And that's just how she said it. In that calm, principal, educator voice, "Scott, why don't you let me help you?" The calmer she got, the angrier I got. By now, I've got Tupperware dating back to 1967 all over the kitchen floor. It's everywhere. I then stand up, give a boot to one of the plastic bowls, and say, "It's not worth it. Forget it." And I walk away.

Pretty stupid, isn't it? Angry over Tupperware. Of course, it was stupid. But let's face it, a lot of the stuff we get angry over is pretty stupid. A few minutes later Marti came in and said, "Now, why don't you tell me what's really going on?"

And that was the perfect question. The truth is that I was angry over some other things going on in my life, and I had failed to acknowledge that, even to myself. That little episode in the kitchen wasn't about Tupperware at all. Rather, I was attempting to blame someone or something else for my unacknowledged anger. It's so easy to blame our spouse. Blame our boss. Blame the government. Blame our parents. Blame our teachers. Blame the church. Blame Tupperware. And I need to say this today even though it's hard for me to say it. Some of us have spent a lot of energy in our lives blaming other people for our unhappiness. There's only one person responsible for your anger—it's you! And God invites us to take a big, powerful, giant spiritual step forward by acknowledging our anger and becoming responsible for it.

And it's only then that we can move to the third word I want to offer today, and that's the word *forgiveness*. At a certain point we cannot live unless we can first forgive. We can only heal with it, if we find courage to deal with it. We cannot move on, unless we can learn to let go. And for many of us, we'll continue to live in our private inferno until we can forgive and let go.

Our Lord understood this. Even when he was being crucified, he found the breath to say, "Father, forgive them, they know not what they do." And when we pray his prayer, "Forgive us our sins, even as we forgive those who sin against us," we are aspiring to the goal of being a forgiving person. Is it easy? No. Is it essential to being a healthy person? Yes. Is it at the heart of being a Christian? Absolutely.

One reason why I think it's so hard to forgive is that when we're angry, we feel like we're justified with our anger, that our circumstances give us permission to be angry, that it's all right in this case to hold the grudge, to seek the revenge, to withhold our support. But could I ask you, if a sinless and innocent man being crucified could forgive his killers, don't you think there might be a way for his followers to forgive others?

I saw a remarkable picture in the *New York Times*. It was a photograph of a black man standing inside a church sanctuary. He was holding hands with a white young man, about seventeen years old; his name was Shawn. What's remarkable was that the black man is the pastor of that church. And the sanctuary they were standing in was partially burned to the ground. And the young white man? Well, he was the confessed arsonist who started the fire. That pastor, along with the leaders and members of his church, had joined hands with Shawn, were praying for him, and were forgiving him for this heinous hate crime. It was an unforgettable picture of forgiveness.

Maybe it doesn't apply, I don't know, but could it be that there is someone, living or dead, to whom you finally need to say, "I forgive you," and then get on with your life? Maybe the relationship can be repaired or maybe it will have to be released. Is it time to finally forgive the company? The church? The school? The country of some wrong done? Regardless, is it time this morning, is it possible this morning that you need to say to your anger, "Enough is enough"? It's important to realize that we all have the power to author and re-author our lives, how we feel, how we behave, how we speak. And that is especially true of anger. Anger is natural and a part of life, but what we finally do with it is our script to write.

Acknowledgment. Responsibility. Forgiveness. None of these words are easy. That's an understatement. They're demanding, challenging, powerful words. Yet the Christian faith not only gives us a gift, but it also demands something of us, too. Acknowledgment. Responsibility. Forgiveness. What I really wanted this morning was to use these three words and come up with some catchy little acronym that would help you in this crash course on anger. But all it spells is *A—R—F*. ARF! ARF! Acknowledgment. Responsibility. Forgiveness. ARF! Don't let anger *dog* your life.

Questions for Reflection

1. What is it that makes you most angry during the course of a week?

2. Can you name a time when you expressed your anger in a positive way? Can you recall a time when you used anger negatively? Looking back on it, how could you re-script that scene in a more positive way?

3. Have you ever had to forgive someone? Was it hard? How did it feel when you finally let go of your anger?

17

The Breathlessly Waiting Blessing

Scripture Text—Matthew 5:1–12

When Jesus saw the crowds, he went up the mountain; and after he sat down, his disciples came to him. Then he began to speak, and taught them, saying: "Blessed are the poor in spirit, for theirs is the kingdom of heaven. Blessed are those who mourn, for they will be comforted. Blessed are the meek, for they will inherit the earth. Blessed are those who hunger and thirst for righteousness, for they will be filled. Blessed are the merciful, for they will receive mercy. Blessed are the pure in heart, for they will see God. Blessed are the peacemakers, for they will be called children of God. Blessed are those who are persecuted for righteousness' sake, for theirs is the kingdom of heaven. Blessed are you when people revile you and persecute you and utter all kinds of evil against you falsely on my account. Rejoice and be glad, for your reward is great in heaven, for in the same way they persecuted the prophets who were before you."

Biblical Reflections

This scripture reading is one of the best known and loved in the entire Bible. However, although the words might have a ring of familiarity, the meaning of these beatitudes remains deep and elusive.

Most of us think of these as ideal attitudes Jesus was encouraging people to possess. For example, we should achieve meekness. We should become hungry and thirsty for righteousness. We should strive to be pure.

And in a sense, it is true that these attitudes are admirable. But in the sermon I take a much different road. Rather than seeing these characteristics in the imperative, that is, here is what you should become, I follow the direction of the indicative. That is to say, Jesus is actually describing situations people were living in and then masterfully applying grace to the situation.

As I have said before, one good question to ask while reading the Bible is *What claim is made about God in the reading?* Applying this question to this particular reading, I see a God who refuses to abandon people, even when they are in the most difficult circumstances. There is good news for the persecuted. There is good news for the meek. There is good news for the pure in heart. The Jesus presented by Matthew is offering insight and grace to people of all circumstances.

I would encourage you to compare this reading with the one found in Luke 6:17ff. The reading is much different, reminding us that the Gospel writers shaped and crafted their material about Jesus to address the needs of their congregations. They were not writing mere biographies of Jesus; they were theologically committed pastors addressing the daily demands of Christians. This is, of course, what every preacher should try to do each Sunday from the pulpit.

Sermon Text

There's a *Peanuts* cartoon I saw a few years ago, and I really liked it. In this cartoon Snoopy is sitting on top of his famous red dog house with his typewriter. Lucy comes along and, as usual, has some advice for him.

She says, "You know what you should do? You should write some personal letters. Then, years from now, they'll publish a book collection of all your personal and intimate correspondence. You might even write some of them to me. That would be fascinating."

Snoopy thinks for a minute. Bends down to his typewriter and types out a short letter: "Dear Lucy, How have you been? Snoopy."

He hands the letter to Lucy, and she just goes crazy. She starts waving her arms and yelling at him. "'How have you been?' What kind of letter is that?!! Nobody would read a dumb letter like that!" She throws the piece of paper at the confounded dog and walks away.

The last frame shows Snoopy typing one more line on that letter. "P.S. Forget it!"

Have you ever had one of those "P.S. Forget it!" moments? One of those moments when you wanted something or needed something or one of those moments when you wanted to offer something of yourself, but it just didn't work, didn't connect, didn't happen?

Maybe it was when you fixed a nice dinner for your family, and you really went to a lot of trouble. You bought the best meat and selected the freshest vegetables. You even used a luscious dessert recipe you found in Martha Stewart's new cookbook. I mean, you really poured yourself into this dinner. You dusted off the best china, ironed the pretty tablecloth, even bought some fresh flowers for the table.

And then you sat down. And people started eating. And they ate like they were using shovels instead of silverware. And instead of enjoying the dinner, people gobbled it down like a Happy Meal and then hurried off to their other activities. What you wanted, you see, was a little lingering time, a little conversation time. You wanted a little human touch with the dinner and not the mere consumption of food. And you also wanted someone, anyone, to look you right in the eye and say, "You really went to a lot of trouble. This dinner is fabulous. Thank you." But instead, you sat there at the table, the dishes dirty, everyone gone, and thought to yourself, "P.S. Forget it!"

My guess is we all have had some "P.S. Forget it!" moments—at home, at work, at church. Those moments when we've wanted at least to be noticed, appreciated, valued. And the reason those moments are so hard for us is that in our "P.S. Forget it!" times, we feel as if we've been forgotten. Even forgotten by God.

And that's really the genius of these so-called "beatitudes."

Let me offer you just a little biblical insight this morning. For years I've preached sermons on this Bible text, all from the perspective that these are attitudes Jesus is commanding us to have as Christians. I've encouraged people to be "poor in spirit" or to be "meek" or to be "hungry for righteousness." And the sermons were okay, but I now realize that is not what this text is about at all.

These so-called "beatitudes" are not commands of Jesus. They are not some Christian attitude checklist. And they are not life goals we should aspire to achieve. The grammar of this theology is indicative, not imperative. Jesus isn't telling people what they should do. He is offering a gift of what God will do. What you find here is an astonishing set of "blessings." A blessing is the surprising gift of God's presence, which is given to us when we find ourselves in a specific situation.

Therefore, Jesus really is saying, "If you are one of those people who are poor in spirit, one of those people who have had the breath knocked out of you by some event in life, don't worry. Don't despair. God will not abandon you or leave. Don't worry. Don't give up—even if your life energy feels like it's running on empty, because even people feeling like that will not be forgotten by God."

Or Jesus says, "If you are one of those meek people in the world, you who never seem to get the spotlight, never make a splash, never get the headline, you who are the quiet and shy and unassuming of this world, don't worry. Don't despair, because even though you may have moments when you feel that you've been forgotten, don't worry, because God will never forget you."

"And some of you who mourn," says Jesus, "you who have had losses that have been devastating to you, you who have had bitter disappointments, you who have had failures, all of you who grieve over your mistakes. I'm speaking to all of you who mourn for what life could have been, should have been, might have been. Don't give up. Don't despair. I will bless you even in your mourning."

And you know, Jesus might even say to some of our teenagers with all their pressures and choices in this world, "You who are choosing to be pure in heart and body, you who are choosing not to drink or smoke pot at the party, you who are choosing to make responsible choices with your sexuality, you who may feel a little lonely at times and a little weird at times and a little outside the circle of peer acceptability at times, don't worry. Don't give up. Stay true to your convictions, because in your situation of trying to be true to your highest ideals, God will bless you."

Do you see what's going on? Jesus is saying that if you find yourself in these situations—situations that at times make us feel like saying, "P.S. Forget it!"—we are not forgotten. There is one who remains with us, who promises us blessing.

Now, granted, seeing that blessing and feeling that blessing while we're in one of those "P.S. Forget it!" moments is sometimes a monumental challenge. It takes faith. And courage. And it also takes a kind of moral imagination. But it can be done.

The poet Emily Dickinson put it like this:

> I never saw a moor,
> I never saw the sea,
> Yet know I how the heather looks,
> And what a wave must be.
>
> I never spoke to God,
> Nor visited in heaven,
> Yet certain am I of the spot
> As if a chart were given.

And what she meant by that, writing from her upstairs bedroom in Amherst, Massachusetts, is that, although she had never visited the spectacular coastline of Cape Cod, she could imagine it. She could experience as real its rolling heather and its crashing waves. And, in the same way, she had never seen God, and she had never visited heaven, but she could imagine as real her divine blessing. Poets are so related to faith because to use the imagination is a profound act of believing.

And that, I think, is what is called for when we are in a "P.S. Forget it!" moment of life. In those moments God waits breathlessly to bless us. But to touch that blessing and to feel that blessing almost always require of us some faith, some courage, some imagination to see that God is coming close.

I don't know, maybe God does speak directly to certain chosen people in this world, maybe it is that literal. But in my experience, what I have witnessed again and again are people who find, in the midst of their mournfulness or impoverishment or whatever their situation, that there is some divine blessing that just shows up. It just shows up. A letter from a friend just shows up. A card from a fellow worker just shows up. A compliment from a boss just shows up. A reassuring word from a doctor just shows up. A door that had been closed for years just opens up. A storm-tossed family has one night—at least one night of peace—and it just shows up.

Now, with one set of eyes you can choose to see it all as coincidence, the flat unfolding of events. Or you can use another set of eyes, the eyes of faith and the eyes of imagination, and see that in your "P.S. Forget it!" moment, God has come close to you through these people or through these events or even through your own solitude. God has come close, and God has blessed you.

I want to tell you a story this morning. It's a true story. A few years ago the Ku Klux Klan made a decision to hold a rally on the steps of the capital building in Indianapolis. I think everything the KKK stands for—hate, intimidation, violence—is absolutely reprehensible. When their rally was announced ministers from all over the city wrestled with what our response should be. We could have shown up at the rally and tried to yell louder than they were yelling, but that would have played right into their need for attention and would have given them free publicity.

What was finally decided was that we would put together a service of community unity. We had blacks and whites, Hispanics and Asians, we had Christians and Jews and Muslims. And rather than reacting against the negative, we wanted to create a night of positive celebration.

Hundreds of us gathered at North Methodist Church on 38th Street and Meridian. The turnout from the community was spectacular. We sang. We prayed. We had different speakers.

But the one speaker I remember the most, the one I will never forget, was an older adult. He was introduced as a Jewish survivor of the Holocaust. This Jewish man spoke quietly from that Christian pulpit. He told of being in the concentration camp. He told of fear and hunger. He told the stories of death. He told us all what we knew but needed to hear again, namely, that hate and violence cannot be tolerated, that we cannot morally be silent.

And then in dramatic fashion he raised both his arms into the air. He said words I will remember my whole life: *I am a survivor. I am a survivor by God's help.*

Immediately, every person in that great sanctuary rose to their feet and exploded in applause. And it went on and on and on. And what I realized was that we weren't just applauding for him. We were applauding his message, his powerful testimony about God's work in this world. We were applauding that part in all of us that wants to survive.

I went up to him after the service and thanked him for his message. I reached out my hand. He reached out his hand toward mine. And as his sleeve rode up his arm slightly, I saw it—just above his wrist, four numbers that had been tattooed on his body. ID numbers from a Nazi concentration camp.

I will never forget him. If ever anyone had the right to throw up his hands and say, "P.S. Forget it!"—it was him. But he didn't. And more than that, he knew that the only way to survive was finally to rely on a spiritual blessing beyond his own strength, but deeply within him.

Here he was, a Jew. Inside this great cathedral. Yet he had spoken to me about God in a way that has far outshone most of the Christian sermons I've ever heard—or probably delivered. He surprised me. Because through him, his words and that handshake, God had come close to me, and God had blessed me.

Jesus was not saying from that mountaintop that you'd better get your life in shape if you want God to bless you. That's what we might say. Jesus wasn't saying you'd better improve or I'm going to punish you. Nor was he suggesting that the way to God was climbing the ladder of moral perfection. That's not, at least here in the Sermon on the Mount, what he's saying. He was saying, "Whatever your situation, whatever your challenge, whatever your circumstance, you can live, you can survive, you are valued, you are not forgotten. Because God blesses you where you are living."

Even when you feel like saying, "P.S. Forget it!"

Questions for Reflection

1. Have you ever had a "P.S. Forget it!" moment in your Christian life?

2. What beatitude do you most connect with as you read the text from Matthew?

3. Have you ever had a situation in life that took a great deal of strength just to survive? What was it, and how did your faith help you through it?

18

Easter Through the Eyes
of a Child

Scripture Text—Luke 24:1–12

But on the first day of the week, at early dawn, they came to the tomb, taking the spices that they had prepared. They found the stone rolled away from the tomb, but when they went in, they did not find the body. While they were perplexed about this, suddenly two men in dazzling clothes stood beside them. The women were terrified and bowed their faces to the ground, but the men said to them, "Why do you look for the living among the dead? He is not here, but has risen. Remember how he told you, while he was still in Galilee, that the Son of Man must be handed over to sinners, and be crucified, and on the third day rise again." Then they remembered his words, and returning from the tomb, they told all this to the eleven and to all the rest. Now it was Mary Magdalene, Joanna, Mary the mother of James, and the other women with them who told this to the apostles. But these words seemed to them an idle tale, and they did not believe them. But Peter got up and ran to the tomb; stooping and looking in, he saw the linen cloths by themselves; then he went home, amazed at what had happened.

Biblical Reflections

The title for this sermon comes not from the biblical text, but from my opening story in the sermon. There is, however, something childlike about the Easter story. In Luke's Gospel especially, the women play a significant role. Luke more than any other gospel writer elevates the role of women. They are the ones who endure with Jesus. They are the ones

119

who discover the resurrection. They are the ones who are the first evangelists. And their experience of the risen Lord is sacred, mysterious, numinous.

In this particular sermon, I'm wanting people to open up to the essence of God's resurrecting presence. That's what happens in this biblical text. People are opened up! Opening up is another way of speaking about faith. The more open we become, the more of God's presence we discover. Too many of us live closed, tight, shut off, and shut down. But make no mistake about it, opening up takes courage. It takes curiosity. It takes a willingness to risk surprise. That's what the resurrection was all about—surprise and grace.

Some approach the resurrection as if it is a proof that Jesus was divine. And that may be true. But the point of resurrection is not to prove something about Jesus; it is about offering the presence of God to me and to you. In the sermon I try to offer something special so that people might walk away having experienced Easter rather than having it explained.

Sermon Text

Well, I want to begin this morning by telling you a conversation I overheard a few weeks ago.

I was working out at the fitness center where I go, and there were two women using the exercise bikes. I was a few feet away using the treadmill. Now, I know you're not supposed to eavesdrop, but when you're working out it gets kind of boring. Plus, I've found I get a lot of good sermon material by overhearing conversations.

Anyway, I was pluggin' along on the treadmill, and I heard one of the women say, "I don't think I'll ever get this body back in shape."

The other one laughed and said, "Yeah, everything I've got is goin' south." I don't know what she meant by that, but I'm not going to touch it this morning.

And then they started laughing, and one of them began telling the story of how her little girl got in bed with her. While she was there, the little girl noticed her mother's stretch marks. You give birth to a couple of babies, and these things happen. Evidently the little girl was looking at her mother's body, touching it, and said quite innocently, "I like the *decorations* on your belly, mommy."

Only through the eyes of a child....

Let me give you a few questions this morning that might help you touch the essence of Easter:

When was the last time you had an experience of awe?

When was the last time you had a moment of wonder and grace?

When was the last time you had spontaneous, ecstatic joy in your life?
When was the last time you felt deeply alive?
When recently have you felt mysteriously connected to God?
When was the last time you felt at one with the universe?

Now, you may be thinking, "Wow, he's finally lost it this morning." Or you may be saying, "Well, I don't know. I mean, I'm just trying to make it day to day. I don't know anything about this mystical stuff." Or you may even be more skeptical, "Yeah, easy for you to say. Live in the *real world* for a few days and then we'll see how much you talk about spontaneous, ecstatic joy."

I read about the real world in Luke's Gospel. I read about slander. I read about mockery. I read about the killing of an innocent man. That's the real world. Just as real as our shootings or Klan rallies or plane crashes. And I read about the friends of Jesus being scared. I read about some who deny ever knowing him. I read about some who curse him behind his back. That's the real world. I read about Mary Magdalene, who felt as if she had lost her very best friend on earth. I read about a mother who watched her son be nailed to a cross and die. And I read about a few close companions, all women actually, who got up on a Sunday morning to go and visit the cemetery. That's the real world, as real, as tragic as our headlines today.

On that first Easter, they went to his tomb with the eyes of adults, but they left with the eyes of children. The miracle of transformation takes place. Peter and John ran breathlessly to the tomb to see if it was so, to see if indeed the wonder and awe and spontaneous ecstatic joy of resurrection was true. And Mary Magdalene, well, her adult eyes could only see grief and funeral-home endings. When this man spoke to her from the tomb, she thought he was the gardener, and all she could imagine was that someone had taken the body of Jesus. Notice that she couldn't see Jesus. He was there. He was not in the tomb. He was there. But with her adult eyes she could not see him or experience him. It was only a few minutes later when she heard this "gardener" say to her, "Mary," that she saw, that she knew, that she had this moment of awesome, wonderful, spontaneous, ecstatic joy. Suddenly she was touched by this mystical peace.

Only through the eyes of a child....

You'll be glad to know that Jesus made the headlines this Easter week: *U. S. News and World Report*—"In Search of Jesus." *Newsweek*—"Rethinking the Resurrection." *Time*—"The Search for Jesus." All three articles are complete with full-cover art work.

Personally, I was glad to see the articles. Each of them was a presentation about the most recent biblical scholarship regarding Jesus, the four

Gospels, and, of course, the resurrection. I don't think we should be afraid of that scholarship. In fact, just the opposite. Real biblical scholarship doesn't hurt faith; it enhances faith. Now, the facts of biblical scholarship may require that we change some ways of thinking about our faith, but that's not bad. That's called growth.

You see, the mistake some of us make is that we assume that the faith we got as a child is the faith we should defend as an adult. Some of us are thirty, forty, fifty years old, but we're still living with our kindergarten faith. And the truth is there's scholarship out there that can help our faith, make us ask harder questions, explore different perspectives. Granted, it's not always simple. Yet, in the long run, the biggest threats to our faith are not the complex questions, but the simplistic answers for which we settle and, by the way, which a lot of churches out there are peddling like cotton candy at the state fair.

Only through the eyes of a child....

I want to suggest to you this morning that there's a difference between a *childlike* faith and a *childish* faith. A childish faith stays the same, gets defensive, never grows. A childish faith hangs out on the door a DO NOT DISTURB sign. But a childlike faith is living life with the capacity to experience God's wonder and grace wherever it may be found. "I like the decorations on your belly, mommy." That's the childlike faith. It's living with the capacity to see that even stretch marks are little signs of God's birthing and rebirthing in this world.

And that's what Mary Magdalene experienced on that first Easter. Did you notice that there is no explanation of *how* Jesus was resurrected? If you read all four accounts of the crucifixion and resurrection, you would notice differences and discrepancies. It's fine to ask the hard questions. The questions of biblical scholarship. That's part of an adult faith. Go ahead, read *Time* or *Newsweek* or *U. S. News and World Report.* I don't agree with everything in the articles, but it's okay. Go ahead and ask some of the puzzling questions.

But after we ask those questions, we've got to come back around and look at the story with the eyes of a child. It's a *simple* faith, but not a *simplistic* one.

The philosopher Paul Ricoeur calls it finding a *second naivete.* That is to say, we start with the wonder of a child, sort out the tough questions of faith as an adult, but then come back around to see the wonder and awe of God in our daily experience. To get caught on the tough questions is a mistake. But to never get to them is a mistake, too. We need the second naivete!

I have a friend who worked as an engineer on the Grand Coulee dam. This is truly an engineering marvel. What I find interesting is that the engineer in him can talk about the technical dimensions of the project, the challenges of building such a large dam, and he can certainly analyze the dam from a critical perspective. But as he talks about it I notice that his eyes sparkle, his voice pauses for a moment, and then he says something like, "You know, it's really incredible. It's, well, it's hard to put into words." And when he says that I know he's looking at it from the eyes of a child.

Mary found in her experience the presence of the resurrected Christ. She found in her experience this mystical presence of God. She found in her experience awe and wonder and joy and grace and aliveness. She didn't need explanations or proofs or arguments. And it's true, she had her real-world problems, too. But what she found on that first Easter morning was that there is a world more real than the real world. It's the world of God's living spirit.

Only through the eyes of a child....

I love the story that Fred Craddock tells of a young minister who went to the hospital to visit a very sick church member. She was barely conscious, mouth gaped open, breathing heavily.

The young man said to her, "I'm the minister from the church. May I help you with anything?" No response. Just the heavy sighs.

He took her hand, bent down toward her ear, and said, "May I say a little prayer with you?"

The woman opened her eyes and said, "Yes, please."

He said, "What do you want me to pray?"

She said, "Pray for my complete recovery."

He looked at the woman, saw her dire condition, and knew there was no way she would ever completely recover. But he did his best, "Dear God, please let this dear woman be healed and recover. May your Holy Spirit be with her totally and completely today."

And before he even got to the "Amen," the woman shot straight up in bed, flashed a big smile, and said, "I feel much better. Thank you."

The minister was shocked. He staggered out of the hospital room like a fighter out of the ring, got to the elevators, looked up at God, and said, "Don't you *ever* do that to me again!"

Only through the eyes of a child....

Some of you are here today, and you do have some real-world problems. Not being able to pay your bills is real. Having a sick child is real. Getting laid off from your job is real. Being hurt by a friend is real. The loneliness of outliving many of your friends is real. But to believe in Easter is to believe that God is more real than the real world you are going through. And sometimes it takes the eyes of a child to see that.

I came out of the sanctuary a few weeks ago, and there was a little girl out in the lobby. She must have been five or six years old, and she was just twirling around and dancing. I couldn't hear any music, but somehow she was hearing it. There she was in the middle of the narthex—joyful, alive, and spontaneously dancing. I loved it!

Frankly, I contrast that with what I see some days in this sanctuary. We sit stiff. Closed. Sometimes a little bored. Looking as if we've heard it all before. Not really expecting to feel much. Maybe not even wanting to feel much. We come here out of duty. Obligation. We don't so much believe in the flowing life of resurrection as we believe in a kind of civil religion. Yes, we have learned to be quite civil.

And believe me, I must confess that it's me, too. Someone said to me a few months ago, "Sometimes you're too serious for your own good." Some days that's probably right. Because I, like you, sometimes lose my childlike eyes. We forget the truth of G. K. Chesterton, who said, "Angels fly because they don't take themselves too seriously." Instead of trusting the positive, I worry about the negative. Instead of finding moments to celebrate, I wait for something to go wrong. Instead of joy, I choose anger. Instead of looking for the empty tombs of this world, I sit back and complain that God doesn't do anything for me.

The best I can tell, there were really two miracles at that first Easter. The first one was that Jesus Christ was resurrected from the dead. That happened 2,000 years ago. Wonderful! But the second was that people like Mary, who had the eyes of a child, saw wonder and awe and, yes, spontaneous, ecstatic joy in their lives. One miracle already has happened and will never be repeated again. The second one—well, that's up to you. It's the miracle that can happen everyday of your life. It's the miracle of seeing the world differently. It's the miracle of finding a new attitude about yourself or others. Easter happened once. That's true. Easter happens again. That's for you! Happy Easter!

Questions for Reflection

1. When was the last time you felt any childlike wonder in your life? Describe the experience.

2. What troubling questions do you have about the resurrection of Jesus?

3. Has God ever really surprised you? When, where, and how?

19

Is That *Really* in the Bible?

Scripture Text—Psalm 25:1–10

To you, O LORD, I lift up my soul. O my God, in you I trust; do not let me be put to shame; do not let my enemies exult over me. Do not let those who wait for you be put to shame; let them be ashamed who are wantonly treacherous. Make me to know your ways, O LORD; teach me your paths. Lead me in your truth, and teach me, for you are the God of my salvation; for you I wait all day long. Be mindful of your mercy, O LORD, and of your steadfast love, for they have been from of old. Do not remember the sins of my youth or my transgressions; according to your steadfast love remember me, for your goodness' sake, O LORD! Good and upright is the LORD; therefore he instructs sinners in the way. He leads the humble in what is right, and teaches the humble his way. All the paths of the LORD are steadfast love and faithfulness, for those who keep his covenant and his decrees.

Biblical Reflections

I selected this psalm because it portrays the Word of God in such a positive way. In my previous book, *Finding a Faith That Makes Sense*, I deal more extensively with the role of the Bible in the life of faith. Over and over again, I find people wanting to use the Bible in a narrow, literalistic, even rigid way. I think this approach to the Bible does damage—not only to the scripture itself, but also to the people trying to interpret it in this way. Yet, the answer to this kind of rigidity is not avoidance of the Bible.

Instead, it is a passionate reaffirmation of it. The psalmist understood that the Word of God does lead us. Our challenge is to find a way of interpreting and listening to the Word of God in a credible and plausible way.

In the sermon, I offer a portrayal of a pastoral conversation I had with a young family. In some ways this conversation is a composite of many conversations I've had through the years. Though in this case, it's an actual couple. I hope the listener to the sermon can hear a central claim, namely, that we need to avoid a literalistic approach to the Bible while at the same time renewing our interest and appreciation of the Bible. That may be a conundrum faced by all mainline Protestant churches these days.

I continue to be amazed at the number of people actually hungry for Bible study experience. This is good, and mainline Protestant churches had better find a way of capitalizing on this interest. But to think of the Bible as some systematic answer book is a mistake of the first order. The Bible represents many books and histories and cultures. The Bible is filled with a variety of perspectives and interpretations of faith. As Christians we seek to interpret the Bible in a way that makes sense in light of the good news of God's love revealed in Jesus Christ.

Sermon Text

You're reading along in the Bible, and you come across a passage of scripture that commands women to learn in silence and be subservient to their husbands, suggesting that the primary role of a woman in society is to have babies. Is that *really* in the Bible?

You turn to one of the psalms of the Old Testament. The psalms are innocent enough, you think, but as you read along you discover a lot of vindictiveness—even a passage that portrays God saying that "the heads of the children should be dashed upon the rocks." Is that *really* in the Bible?

You read about a man having some kind of physical seizure—his body convulsing, crying out desperately. Knowing what you know about medicine, you naturally think he needs to see a doctor. Instead, you read that the problem with this man is that an invisible flying creature, called a demon, has invaded his body, and what he needs is not a hospital but an exorcism. Does your health insurance pay for exorcisms? Is that *really* in the Bible?

You think, "Well, I'll just read the words of Jesus. That will work—just the words of Jesus, written in red, you know." But as you read the words of Jesus, you find things like, "A man must hate his father and mother before he can be my disciple." Hate? Hate of parents? Is that *really* in the Bible?

I'll never forget a conversation I had several years ago. A young couple came into my office. They had been reasonably active in the church, and they came by to tell me that they were leaving the church. On the one hand, I always appreciate conversations of this kind because they help me see how the church might be improved. Unfortunately, what often happens is that people just stop coming to church, and as a minister you're never quite sure what's going on with people. But these folks came by, and we talked. And they were quite blunt about it. They said, "We've got to find a church where they preach the Bible!"

What do we do with the Bible? What place should the Bible have in the life of a church? Is just standing up and quoting verses really preaching the Bible? Is turning the Bible into some answer book really preaching the Bible? Is applying the Bible in a step-one, step-two, step-three format really applying the Bible? And what about those passages in the Bible that just don't make sense? Passages that endorse slavery. Passages that demean women. Passages that support violence. Passages that degrade Jews. What do we do with those passages?

Part of having a dynamic faith—and by dynamic I mean a living, growing, changing faith—is finding a way to connect to the Bible. Obviously, the psalm that we read this morning paints with glorious strokes a God who instructs, teaches, guides—which of course is what the Bible is designed to do. In another place the psalmist writes, "Thy Word is a lamp unto my feet." Yet, how do we light the lamp without its blowing up in our faces? What do we do with the Bible?

Well, I looked at this couple and said, "Let me talk to you for a few minutes about the Bible."

I said, "First of all, you need to know what the Bible is and isn't. Some people have the idea that the Bible was given to us directly by God. Sort of like people were living and suddenly, like the UPS man, God shows up with a package labeled THE BIBLE. No doubt with gold letters and calf-skin leather." "Yes," they said, "But isn't the Bible the inspired Word of God?" Oh, I knew I had my hands full at this point. I love conversations of this kind.

"Well" I said, "it depends upon what you mean by the word *inspiration*. Some people define inspiration as if God came down and literally took the hands of the biblical writers, moved the very pen upon the page—that every single, literal word that flowed through the quill of the pen came from the mind of God. But I don't see it that way. You see, the Bible is both a human book and a divine book. It's human in the sense that men, maybe women, wrote the words, and the words written reflect their human struggle, their human quest to find God, understand God, share God with other people. Their human words reflect their culture. Reflect their thought forms. Reflect their ideologies. And that makes sense to me. For example, it would be unfair to say that the biblical writers were dumb because they didn't believe in electricity. They couldn't believe in electricity before electricity existed, right? Their human words reflect both their understanding and lack of understanding."

The woman said, "Yes, that's right. Electricity hadn't even been discovered yet." I said, "Exactly. The biblical writers wrote their words out of their ancient culture. It's not that God dropped the words down to earth like a package attached to a parachute; it's more like the words grew out of the ground of their human and cultural experience. And since the Bible was written, there have been all kinds of new discoveries in history and science and psychology, and we just can't ignore that."

At that point the man, who was really sincere—fidgeting, but sincere—asked the question, "But how do we know what God wants us to do?"

I said, "That's a perfect question. Though it was written by human beings living in an ancient culture, the Bible still carries with it a divine word, and that word instructs and guides and touches our lives. That's why we need to read the stories of the Bible, not so much to apply them literally to our lives and not so much because every single word of the story is literally true for all time. But as we read the story, we come face to face with the presence of God. And sometimes that presence brings us the comfort of grace, and sometimes that presence brings us the demand of discipleship. But most of all, like saltwater taffy, the Bible stretches the imagination of our faith in God."

I could tell he was struggling with that idea. Most of us, if we've read the Bible at all, have read the Bible to get information. And information is fine. But the real point of reading the Bible is to have our moral imagination stretched. It's the experience of God that really counts.

Did you see what happened in Dallas this past week? In the middle of a school board meeting, a fight broke out. The month before, there was a shouting match that intensified to the point that the new superintendent had to leave the room. Do you see what lack of human imagination that demonstrates?

Last week I spent about an hour at the Museum of Modern Art. I was especially intrigued by the large abstract paintings by Ed Clark. The colors. The bold strokes. The textures. Now, I can't explain those paintings, but after seeing them I experienced my mind and imagination being stretched. It's crucial for the well-being of the world, not to mention our personal lives and our families, to have our moral imagination stretched. That's what reading the Bible can do for us.

But the man sitting across the table emphatically said to me, "Yes, but how do I know what parts of the Bible are ancient culture and what parts of the Bible are the real Word of God?"

That's a good question. At that point, I was fidgeting a bit. What I said was this: "The Bible is like a friend. A conversation partner. And with a friend, we have dialogue. The more you talk with a friend, ask questions, laugh, cry, spend time in quiet with that friend, the more you are deeply connected with that friend. Because the greatest gift a friend can give, unless it's a cash donation of a million dollars, is the gift of listening."

I don't know if he really got it or not, this idea of the Bible as companion. Marti made a comment to me the other day about a couple we enjoy as friends. She said, "Do you know why I really like them as friends? I like them because every time I'm with them, I find myself wanting to know more about them." Haven't you found that to be true? You can meet some people, and after about two minutes you pretty much know all there is to know. But people of real depth are like peeling back an onion; layer after layer after layer of experience is discovered. And the more you talk to them the more you're drawn to them. And that's what I tried to tell this couple sitting in my office. The Bible is like a friend, and the more you get past the surface literalism, the more you have dialogue with the Bible, the more of God's presence you discover. The Bible isn't an answer book. Instead, God reveals God's self in the midst of the dialogue we have with the Bible.

Martin Marty made a great observation in a lecture a couple of weeks ago when he said: "Argument is driven by the quest for an answer. Conversation is driven by the celebration of a question." And that's the role of the Bible in our lives. We're able to bring our questions, our doubts, our joys, our fears. And the more we dialogue with the Bible, the more we discover the living presence of God through the Bible.

Things got kind of quiet in my office after I talked about "dialogue" with the Bible. I was worried. Had I given them too much? Had I confirmed their fear that I was some "liberal" minister? Finally, the wife asked me, "Can you give us an example of what you mean?"

I said, "Let me give you a couple. First of all, there are stories in the Bible that just don't make sense in our daily world. Do you remember when your daughter Jenny was sick with asthma a couple of years ago?" They nodded yes. That had been a traumatic time for their family. The little girl was five years old, and they almost lost her. It was a severe respiratory problem. I said, "How do you understand that problem Jenny experienced?" The mother said, "What do you mean?"

"I mean, what do you think caused the problem?" And the mother replied, "Well, it was just a disease. I mean, she's okay now, with medication. It wasn't anybody's fault."

I looked her right in the eyes and said, "You know there are stories in the Bible that might suggest Jenny's real problem was that a demon had escaped from the pit of hell and invaded her body, and she was sick because a demon did it to her." I asked her, "Do you believe that?" She said, "No. Is that *really* in the Bible?"

"You know, there's another explanation," I said. "Some passages in the Bible might suggest that Jenny was being punished for a sin that either she committed or her mother committed. Do you think God punishes people for their sins like that?" She said, "No, no, I don't believe God does that to people." And I said, "You know, I don't believe God does that to people either. But it's in the Bible. That's why I can't get up on Sundays and quote the Bible here and there, applying the literal words of the Bible. To do that would not only betray the essence of God, it would hurt both of you. It would hurt children like your Jenny."

You'll never guess what that father said next. He looked at his wife, and then he sort of looked down at the table, and then he said to me, "You know, we don't really want to leave the church. We just want our daughter to grow up here and learn about the Bible. Sometimes we don't think the Bible is emphasized enough here at our church."

Finally, I saw through it. They, like all of you, wanted a faith that is alive, a faith that has been nourished from the stories of scripture. They were slightly misguided in that they thought to have a biblical faith meant that it had to be a literalistic, legalistic, fundamentalistic, simplistic faith. But that's not it at all. I tried to help them see that they could have, that you can have, a biblical faith by being in dialogue with scripture—not a textbook to be followed rigidly, but a conversation partner with whom we listen and learn and ask our deepest questions. That's the Bible.

But I also looked at them and said, "You know, I agree with you. I don't think we've studied the Bible in our church the way we should, and I don't think we've taught the stories of faith to our children the way we could. But the answer to not emphasizing the Bible enough is not to emphasize it improperly."

And then I said, "You know, the real key is for each of us to find ways of listening to scripture, not just on the surface, but by making a heart connection to the flow of God's presence that comes to us in the stories of the Bible. Not hung up on the literal/cultural/historical details of the Bible, like snagging our jeans on a barbed-wire fence, but letting the real essence of the story touch our lives. And that means picking up the Bible and reading it. That means attending church regularly. That means getting connected to a study group."

We just sat there for a moment. It had been a great conversation. I was impressed with their honesty. I was both energized and exhausted. I was pleased that God had helped me answer each question with authenticity and integrity. They looked at each other. I looked at them. I said, "When we treat the Bible like that, it is like finding a treasure in a field or discovering a glimmering pearl of great price." She smiled at me and said, "That's in the Bible, isn't it?" I said, "Yes...it *really* is."

Questions for Reflection

1. What view of the Bible, if any, did you grow up with in your home or church?

2. Would you be willing to try an experiment? Try reading the Gospel of Luke, one chapter per day, and then reflect on what difference the Word of God made upon you.

3. Do you know people who try to take a flat, literalistic approach to scripture? What do you think of them and their perspective?

SECTION IV

Edification

20

Why Generations Need Each Other

Scripture Text—Deuteronomy 34:1–12

Then Moses went up from the plains of Moab to Mount Nebo, to the top of Pisgah, which is opposite Jericho, and the LORD showed him the whole land: Gilead as far as Dan, all Naphtali, the land of Ephraim and Manasseh, all the land of Judah as far as the Western Sea, the Negeb, and the Plain—that is, the valley of Jericho, the city of palm trees—as far as Zoar. The LORD said to him, "This is the land of which I swore to Abraham, to Isaac, and to Jacob, saying, 'I will give it to your descendants'; I have let you see it with your eyes, but you shall not cross over there." Then Moses, the servant of the LORD, died there in the land of Moab, at the LORD's command. He was buried in a valley in the land of Moab, opposite Bethpeor, but no one knows his burial place to this day. Moses was one hundred twenty years old when he died; his sight was unimpaired and his vigor had not abated. The Israelites wept for Moses in the plains of Moab thirty days; then the period of mourning for Moses was ended.

Joshua son of Nun was full of the spirit of wisdom, because Moses had laid his hands on him; and the Israelites obeyed him, doing as the LORD had commanded Moses.

Never since has there arisen a prophet in Israel like Moses, whom the LORD knew face to face. He was unequaled for all the signs and wonders that the LORD sent him to perform in the land of Egypt, against Pharaoh and all his servants and his entire land, and for all the mighty deeds and all the terrifying displays of power that Moses performed in the sight of all Israel.

Biblical Reflections

There's hardly a figure in the Bible who exceeds the courage, the insight, the drama of Moses. His very life is a parable of the working of God in the world, reminding each of us that God's purposes are not thwarted by the principalities and powers existing in the world. From Moses' birth to his death God was working in his life, and thus in the life of Israel.

This particular story is poignant because it represents the end of Moses' life. There is such drama in this ending. Yet, I'm intrigued by how much influence Moses continues to exert, even in his old age. Growing older doesn't necessarily mean we have to diminish in our influence of this world.

What does it mean to grow old? And what does it mean to tranfer leadership from one generation to another? This happens all the time in the church, often with stress and strain. Nevertheless, the generations of the faith community need one another. The old man Moses has his role. The young leader Joshua has his role, too. To underestimate either is a serious mistake for the community of faith. In the church today we need the WW II generation, and the Vietnam generation, and the Generation X generation. To miss one another is to impoverish our lives and the life of the church.

Sermon Text

This past spring I had a chance to be in a conference with the poet Maya Angelou. I must tell you that just being in her presence was magical. She read poetry, told stories, sang songs. At one moment she had the audience doubled over with laughter; at other moments we were choking back our tears. But most of all what she did was simply tell the story of her childhood. That's the power of stories in our lives.

When she was a young girl, she was sexually abused by her mother's boyfriend. The man said to her, "If you tell anybody, I'll kill your brother!" She loved and adored her brother. In fact, her brother was one of the most positive people in her childhood and to this day remains one of her best friends. Therefore, she told absolutely no one.

It wasn't long afterward that the man who had violated her was found dead on a deserted street in St. Louis, Missouri. He had been beaten to death over a gambling debt.

When Maya heard about the news of his death, she decided that she would never speak again. You see, in her mind, she believed that it was her anger and rage and voice that had killed the man. She became desperately afraid that if she spoke again her voice might kill someone else. And so, like a tortoise closing up its shell, she retreated into isolation and silence. She didn't speak. For years she did not utter a word.

She was sent to live with an aunt in Stamps, Arkansas. But this aunt was no ordinary woman. She was old and big and powerful, and she carried herself like an Egyptian queen inside that little Arkansas house. And she went to church. Oh, did she go to church! All day on Sunday. And on Monday, she would get ready for church on Tuesday. Wednesday, too. And Saturday was spent getting ready for Sunday.

But more than merely going to church, church filled that house; it became the centerpiece of life. Well, the music of the church was indeed inside that aunt's house. Maya, this wounded, vulnerable, silenced little girl, heard the music. She wouldn't sing it, but she heard it. In her speech she told us, "My whole body became an ear as I listened to my aunt's music. And over and over and over she would tell me, 'You keep listening to that music girl; it'll put starch in your backbone someday.'"

And she told the story of how she would sit in her aunt's bedroom in front of the dresser mirror. Do you remember your mother's dresser? The little perfume bottle? The small jewelry box? The tiny china figurine? Maya would sit there, and her aunt would comb her hair, braid her hair. Stroke after stroke, she combed Maya's thick black hair. And as she combed her hair, this old woman would sing. Church songs. Spiritual songs. Songs of hope and faith and promise. And sometimes she would sing the words:

> Over my head, I hear music in the air.
> Over my head, I hear music in the air.
> Over my head, I hear music in the air.
> There must be a God somewhere.

And those words became a bridge from one generation to another. The old woman saw in the young woman the worth and value that every human person deserves to feel. And that affirmation, without a doubt, had the power to turn the silence of this little girl into the roaring voice of one of our nation's most articulate poets.

Generations—we do need each other, don't we?

I think this reading today from the last chapter of Deuteronomy reflects one of the most poignant moments in the history of Israel. The old man, Moses, goes up to the top of Mount Nebo. Can you imagine the video of history playing through his mind at that moment? All the efforts of liberating his people from Egyptian slavery. All the speeches ending with that same benediction—"Let my people go." All the years of putting up with the wilderness and the whining and the whimsical longing to turn back. Finally, there he is, so close to the promised land that he can see it from the mountaintop. God says, "There it is Moses. There's the land I've been telling you about since Egypt. Take a good look at it Moses." And Moses did look at it. And then he died.

Remarkably, the story is not told with any subplot of bitterness or disappointment. Irony, of course. But there's no story here about God's cheating Moses out of something. Instead, what you find is that Moses and his generation had their place. But waiting in the wings is a young man, Joshua, and he and his generation will now take their place. Without Moses, the nation of Israel would not have gotten to the point of seeing the land. Without Joshua, the nation of Israel would not have gotten to the point of living in the land. Both generations were crucial to the working of God.

One of the gifts that we have in the church community is this gift of the generations. But every gift must be nurtured, and every gift has its challenges.

We live in a society today in which many of our children are flat out in trouble. If it's not poverty, then it's violence. If it's not violence, then it's racism. If it's not racism, then it's drugs. If it's not drugs, then it's this pervasive, pernicious feeling of hopelessness that seems to hold captive so many of the very young. And what's even more alarming is the number of children and teenagers in our society who have no significant relationship with any older adult, including their parents. It's one thing to ask, "Where are the kids?" But it's another to ask, "Where are the adults?"

And just as our young have been disconnected from adults, many of our adults have become either frightened or isolated from the younger generation. I had one woman who confessed to me quite candidly a few months ago that she's scared to go to the mall anymore because of all the teenagers. I'm not suggesting that all teenagers are dangerous. They're not. But can you at least appreciate her perception? For her, the crowd of teenagers going up and down the corridors of consumerism felt threatening, menacing, dangerous.

Yet, there is some song that an older generation needs to sing over the heads of a younger generation. And there is some respectful blessing that needs to flow from a younger generation to an older generation. And that's the opportunity of church. As church we have an opportunity to be either a *mirror* or a *mural* for the generations.

As a *mirror* we can simply be another place in the culture where the isolation of generations is the primary reality. Do you feel the contradiction of that headline I read in one church newsletter a few years ago that read: "ALL CHURCH DINNER SUNDAY… NO CHILDREN UNDER 12 PLEASE"? It is so easy for Generation Xers and Baby Boomers to be suspicious of each other. It's so easy to assume that older adults have nothing more to offer the church. It's way too easy to assume that our children and youth aren't really that interested in the church.

But instead of being a mirror of the culture, maybe we could be a *mural* for the vision of God. Think about it, the community of the church as this great big living picture of different generations learning from each other, worshiping together, blessing one another. And in that mural, we replace generational isolation with conversation, understanding, even with physical touch. And in that mural, we replace fear with the wisdom of experience and the beauty of exuberance. Community demands a lot of openness, but it especially demands a generational appreciation. Recently we interviewed people at University Church, asking the question "What do you most appreciate about the church?" And the answer that surfaced again and again was that people appreciate the bringing together of generations that takes place here. Which is another way of saying, people love genuine community!

But if that's the mural God wants us to paint, how in the world do we begin to paint such a project for the world to see? Well, let me suggest some very practical ideas for composition. You can use them here at the church, but you can also use them at home or at work.

The first one is this: *In the church community, we need to throw out all the stereotypes about age.* That's a great beginning point in order to bring generations together. Let's not assume that old means stale. Some of the most vital, open-minded, forward-thinking people in this church are older adults. Let's not assume that young means immature. Some of the best leaders we have are young chronologically but are mature in spirit. Let's don't assume that student means transient. Some of the people who love this church the most are students who are only here for a short time, but the time they are here is life changing. Let's not assume that youth means uninterested. I've met some of our youth, and they are thoughtful, committed, and deeply interested in this church. And let's not assume that child means unable to comprehend our faith. Some of our children have incredible insights about our faith. When we become a part of this church community, we get rid of the stereotypes!

Second, *we need to encourage each other to redefine age.* It's not so much that you're as young as you feel as it is that you're as vital as you choose to be. I want you really to hear that today—life vitality is a choice of faith! Jesus said, "Those who believe in me, out of them shall flow living water." That was his way of saying that our choice of faith is also a choice of daily life vitality. I know people who are middle aged, at the peak of their careers, who redefine their lives by going into a new field. I know women who are defining their forties in terms of having their first baby. I know retirees who are redefining retirement in terms of productivity, vitality, and service to others. Don't forget, John Glenn is going back into space! Now, don't misunderstand me this morning. I'm not talking about trying to look younger than you really are or pretending that you're something that you're really not. I'm simply suggesting that you don't need to let anyone define for you what it means to be thirty or forty or fifty or sixty or seventy. Was Moses too old to lead Israel? Was Joshua too young to lead Israel? Only you and God should define the vitality of age.

Third, *we need to learn the skill of blessing someone of a different generation*. The point of growing older is not to live a life of complete comfort and ease, surrounded only by people who look and act and think as we do. I mean really, so what if you can play golf every day or go on a cruise every season or vacation in some exotic place year after year? The real test of our growing is what kind of human legacy we are building with people. I really do believe that one of the most important challenges of our growing older, at any age, is reaching out to someone younger.

But that blessing goes both ways. If you are young, then I want to encourage you this morning to reach out to someone older. Not in some condescending way, but a genuine move toward those of a different generation. Seek them out. Pursue their wisdom. Listen to their insights. That kind of generational sharing becomes crucial in our quest for the blessing of God.

Think about it like this: The old man Moses had his time and place. The young man Joshua stood up to face his challenges, too. And both generations then, as now, needed one another.

I thought about the importance of generations and their differences this week when I found a poem by that little girl who moved from silence to speech in Stamps, Arkansas, because someone of a different generation blessed her. In her poem, *Human Family*, Maya Angelou notes the differences in people, people she has seen and met all around the world. She celebrates the uniqueness of each person. Appreciates, not tolerates, but appreciates the rainbow diversity that exists across the spectrum of the human family. Yet, she ends the poem with a profound truth that is essential for every person, indeed, every church to finally grasp. She says, "We are more alike, my friends, than we are unalike."

And I think she is right. For I have found that truth again and again as I have visited the very old and the very young, as I have interacted with black and brown and tan and white, as I have preached to the very poor and the very rich. There is something compelling, attractive, something utterly beautiful in our differences. And I see that in our story about

Moses. He was so old, at the very end of his life's vitality. But even at the end of his life it is so clear that his presence mattered. Yes, *he* mattered.

There is such tremendous power in recognizing what we have in common. Don't let the wrinkles on the skin or the color of the hair or the youthfulness of the eyes determine the community you experience. We need each other. We really do. Because, as Moses found in Joshua and Joshua found in Moses, we are "more alike, my friends, than we are unalike." And that truth is worth learning at any age. It's worth learning today.

Questions for Reflection

1. Name a significant older person in your life. Why does that person mean so much to you?

2. How might you be able to bless someone from another generation?

3. Have you felt the tensions among the generations in your church? If so, why do those tensions exist, and how can the church create more appreciation between generations?

21

The Partnership
of Ministry

Scripture Text—Philippians 4:10–20

I rejoice in the LORD *greatly that now at last you have revived your concern for me; indeed, you were concerned for me, but had no opportunity to show it. Not that I am referring to being in need; for I have learned to be content with whatever I have. I know what it is to have little, and I know what it is to have plenty. In any and all circumstances I have learned the secret of being well-fed and of going hungry, of having plenty and of being in need. I can do all things through him who strengthens me. In any case, it was kind of you to share my distress.*

You Philippians indeed know that in the early days of the gospel, when I left Macedonia, no church shared with me in the matter of giving and receiving, except you alone. For even when I was in Thessalonica, you sent me help for my needs more than once. Not that I seek the gift, but I seek the profit that accumulates to your account. I have been paid in full and have more than enough; I am fully satisfied, now that I have received from Epaphroditus the gifts you sent, a fragrant offering, a sacrifice acceptable and pleasing to God. And my God will fully satisfy every need of yours according to his riches in glory in Christ Jesus. To our God and Father be glory forever and ever. Amen.

Biblical Reflections

Philippians is one of my favorite books of the apostle Paul. Certainly, there are some memorable passages. Additionally, there is something tender about it as he sounds the note of friendship again and again. But more than a note of friendship, what is at stake in this letter is the financial support of Paul's ministry. Not surprisingly, there is an intimate connection between money and ministerial success. This church had been supportive of Paul's ministry, both spiritually and financially. But now due to his imprisonment, this support is teetering in a different direction.

In the sermon, I try to say to the congregation that as a minister I want a vital partnership with them. I don't want to live a model of minister as dictator. Nor do I want a model of minister as errand boy. Somewhere in between there is the vitality and passion of partnership. Many churches are in crisis as they relate to their ministers. The model of partnership means that both sides are responsible, both are indispensable, and together each is stronger in the partnership of ministry. By the way, after I preached this sermon, I had a young couple come up to me and say, "We're ready to go! You can count on us to be your partners!" I was thrilled. I don't know of a minister who wouldn't be thrilled to hear those words from someone in his or her congregation.

Sermon Text

The chairman of the board at the church of Philippi was fidgeting. The board meeting was running long. The Christian education division was in a crisis; two Sundays ago the four-year-olds broke open a box of crayons and started coloring on the walls. The property committee was reporting that at least three people were threatening to become Presbyterians if something wasn't done about the temperature in the sanctuary. You know, just normal church business.

But board chairpersons sometimes know what the rest of you do not know. Sometimes they carry burdens heavier than the earth itself. Sometimes that's why they fidget.

The chairman cleared his throat at the end of the meeting, not once, but twice. His voice sounded shaky when he began, "I have some difficult news to share with you. Our missionary, Paul, the one we loved so much, the one we've been supporting financially, the one who has been starting new churches all over Europe, the one who has been our personal missionary and friend—well, folks, there's no easy way to say this. Paul has been thrown into prison."

Suddenly a collective gasp went up from the church parlor. For a moment, the news stunned all of them, no one knowing what to say, how to feel, what to do.

One of the dear ladies on the board started to cry.

One of the elders asked, "Well, is there anything we should be doing for him?"

Another person jumped up and said, "I don't care if he is in jail. He's still our missionary, and I think we should support him!"

But there were others. Others rose from their chairs, faces beet red with anger, spitting words of fire. "If we keep sending money to that jailbird, that impostor of a minister, I will never give another penny to this church!"

Someone else yelled from the back of the room, "Our minister is a disgrace!"

Now do you see why board chairpersons sometimes fidget?

There is no relationship, is there, quite like the relationship between a minister and a congregation? At times, it can be one of the most meaningful and satisfying relationships in our lives. Powerful. Positive. Healthy. At other times, however, it can disintegrate, becoming devastating, deadly, divisive.

What does a quality relationship between a minister and congregation look like? What can a church do to make that relationship better? What responsibilities do ministers have to make the relationships with their churches quality relationships?

All of those questions are really lurking behind the scenes in this little book we call Philippians. Paul had entered into an agreement with the Philippian church. It wasn't a signed contract per se, but it was a binding legal agreement in the Roman world called *consensual societas*. It was an unsigned but legal agreement between two parties.

And in Paul's case, the agreement worked like this—Paul would do his missionary work by preaching and starting churches, and in return the Philippian congregation would send him regular financial support. Pretty simple, right? Well, it was simple until Paul was thrown into prison. And as soon as that happened, there were those who said, "Wait just a minute. Paul's not out preaching the gospel anymore. He's in jail. And since he's not preaching the gospel anymore, we have no more obligation or relationship toward him."

Paul tries to move the Philippian Christians to a deeper place of understanding. The relationship of minister and church is really a partnership. Partnership. In partnership, both sides are important. In partnership, both sides make contributions. In partnership, both sides have responsibilities.

Now, I wonder this morning, what would it mean if you and I started to create more and more partnership in our relationship?

Well, it would, first of all, mean that the role of the senior minister in this church is not to be *dictatorial ruler*. Though some days that's awfully tempting. My job isn't to rule this church. My job isn't to dictate what this church will do or not do in its future. Yes, I have ideas and experience and expertise around what it means to be an effective church, and I want to offer that again and again. As a partner I feel as if I am called to shape the future of this church. But if all I do is demand and dictate, pretty soon this becomes *my* church and not *our* church. Partnership is always a two-way street.

And if partnership is important, it also means the role of senior minister in this church is not to be *passive pastor.* And some days that's tempting, too. Because when you're passive what you're really doing is abdicating responsibility. There's a part of all of us that wants to let someone else be responsible for the church.

Some ministers take the posture "Whatever the people want to do, that's what we'll do. Whatever the committee comes up with, that's what we'll implement. Whatever direction the board pulls out of the hat this month, that's where we'll go."

But can you understand that sometimes people and committees and boards need leadership from their ministers? Offering ideas. Painting possibilities. Pointing toward a vision. And let's not forget that sometimes ministers have to remind people of the fundamental claims of the gospel upon their lives. That's the vitality of partnership. In fact, it's a pretty good rule of thumb that if you find a minister relating to the congregation in a passive way, then there is some deep problem happening.

If partnership is to be vital at University Christian Church, that also means that the role of the senior minister is not to be *spiritual superstar.* I know that over the last few weeks I've received a lot of attention. That happens to the new minister, I suppose. I appreciate that, and all of it makes me feel very welcome here. But what I know is that we have people on this church staff who have been here for years. They have gifts and talents and abilities, and they are doing exceptional ministry. I am a partner with them.

And I know that this congregation, maybe more than any other Disciples church in the country, has a wealth of gifts and talents and abilities, and that you, the people of this church, are doing real ministry. I saw real ministry this week when members of the Bible Discovery Class and the staff from our Week-Day School moved toward a family in their most desperate time. It was genuine, beautiful, authentic ministry. Helping a young family pick up the pieces of their lives is real ministry. And it happened because of partnership.

Sometimes we get caught up in the misconception that the job of laypeople is to "help the minister out." But that's not it at all. In fact, if anything, my job is to help you out, help you find your gifts, discover your ministry, unleash your unique caring out into the world. That's the kind of ministry that isn't subordinate to any senior minister. It's real ministry.

It is this deeper feeling of partnership that Paul calls the Philippian Christians to embrace. Peppered throughout these four chapters are references to their "sharing" with one another, their "gratefulness" for one another, their mutual "giving and receiving" with each other. Embodied in Paul's very experience was the knowledge that the relationship of minister and congregation transcends mere legalistic interpretation of some social agreement. It goes beyond the mere economics of supply and demand. Finally, ministry embodies the beauty and challenge of being partners together in the life of God.

But it's never easy.

Henry Ward Beecher was one of the greatest preachers in American history. For many years, he was senior minister of one of New York's largest and most prestigious churches. However, as is always the case, not everyone in his congregation was a Beecher supporter. There was one woman in the congregation who absolutely gave him fits. A criticism here. A personal attack there. It was well known that this was not a happy relationship between pastor and parishioner.

Finally, Reverend Beecher went to make a call on the lady to see if there was any way they could iron out their differences. He went to the door, knocked gently, but no one answered. He knocked a little harder, but still no one came to the door. Now, he knew she was in there. (Remember, we ministers know you're in there!) But she just wouldn't come to the door.

He then got down on his knees, looked through the keyhole, and what did he see but another big eye staring right back at him. Beecher started laughing. The woman on the other side of the door started laughing. And his only comment was, "This is the first time in years we've seen eye to eye, and we had to get down on our knees to do it!"

Partnership between minister and church is not easy. Being a dictator is easy. Being passive is easy. Being a superstar, in a way, is easy. But to believe in the gifts and talents of one another, to believe the best about one another, to support one another, to work hard at understanding one another, to set aside our own desires for the well-being of the entire church, that's not easy. In the next few weeks, you're going to have the opportunity to be partners with this church through raising your level of giving. That's not easy either. But it's this supportive, synergistic partnership that God calls us to live.

And I don't think it's any coincidence that in this same book of Philippians, in chapter two, we find one of the greatest biblical summaries of the meaning of Christ in the world. "Christ," writes Paul, "had equality with God, but he did not look upon this equality as something to be desperately clutched with white-knuckled fury. Instead, he became a human partner with all people, experiencing the breadth and depth of the human drama, including his own death." Paul envisions here a remarkable divine partnership. Christ in this world wants to be a spiritual partner in the challenges of our lives.

When we learn how to be partners with one another we become the presence of Jesus Christ in the world. And that's why the partnership that we are now beginning to forge at University Christian Church is so important. Because when it's right, even when you and I have to get down on our knees so we can see eye to eye, then it's really right.

Paul tried to explain that, even though he was in prison, he was still preaching the gospel of Jesus Christ. That his partnership with them had not ceased to exist. Prison just became another place to share in ministry.

That church board must have somehow risen to the occasion because someone, I don't know who it was, someone stood up in the middle of that board meeting and made a motion. "I move that we continue our partnership with our minister, that we send him our financial support, and that our friend Epaphroditus visit Paul in prison."

How important, how strong, how delicate this partnership between church and minister.

Someone seconded the motion. The chairman fidgeted a little more.

Folks, we vote for a relationship with a minister every single day we're a member of a church. We vote for this partnership by how we attend church, by how we participate, by how we give, by the words we speak or don't speak. We vote by our attitudes, by our actions. We vote by the kinds of conversations we have in the parking lot after church.

And I've been thinking a lot about ministers and congregations lately, because as we open a new chapter together in the history of our church, this is what I know: It's not all about *me*. And it's not all about *you*. It's truly all about God in *us*.

Questions for Reflection

1. How might you demonstrate to your minister that you would like to be in partnership?

2. What metaphor might best describe the relationship your minister has with your church?

3. How might the paradigm of partnership be applied in other areas of your life?

22

Don't
Give Up!

Scripture Text—Matthew 15:21–28

Jesus left that place and went away to the district of Tyre and Sidon. Just then a Canaanite woman from that region came out and started shouting, "Have mercy on me, Lord, Son of David; my daughter is tormented by a demon." But he did not answer her at all. And his disciples came and urged him, saying, "Send her away, for she keeps shouting after us." He answered, "I was sent only to the lost sheep of the house of Israel." But she came and knelt before him, saying, "Lord, help me." He answered, "It is not fair to take the children's food and throw it to the dogs." She said, "Yes, Lord, yet even the dogs eat the crumbs that fall from their masters' table." Then Jesus answered her, "Woman, great is your faith! Let it be done for you as you wish." And her daughter was healed instantly.

Biblical Reflections

Surely not Jesus, not sweet Jesus speaking so harshly, so insensitively as he is portrayed speaking in this scripture story! The edge in this story is also what brings forth its meaning. A good rule of thumb when reading the Bible is that the texts and sayings we most resist may be the ones we need to hear the most. The fact that Jesus and this woman match wits is a sign of her faith, even tenacity, as she is on her spiritual search.

Jesus is using an aphorism, a saying, and the use of such an aphorism is not necessarily a sign that Jesus believed it as much as it is a sign that he wanted to use it in the skillful art of conversation. Jesus did not think people were dogs. His use of this proverb enabled the conversation to develop to a point of insight. In the end, this woman's faith is heroic. Rather than putting her down, Jesus enables this woman to discover a depth of faith that would otherwise have been impossible had she been timid and passive.

In the sermon, I address what seems to be a universal need—the need to endure. At some point in life, our journey becomes one of courage or cowardice, strength or weakness, get up and go or sit down and die. Jesus praises this woman for her strength of faith, ah, she keeps circling and circling the divine, and through such endurance there flowed the healing grace of God. It is true. God is grace, but some grace is hard won by tenacity, endurance, and an indefatigable spirit.

Sermon Text

I want to start off today by giving you an image. You see if it connects or not.

The image is of an aquarium. I like aquariums. I find them mesmerizing. You look inside the aquarium, and there are beautiful fish swimming gracefully in the water. Orange and black and red, their colors gleam from the overhead light. You hear the slight hum-hum-hum of the pump. You see the small stream of tiny bubbles rising to the surface. You also see the blue gravel at the bottom, the little mermaid bridge the fish swim under. Maybe you see a snail or two climbing up the side.

And also, essential to every aquarium, you see some plants. They've been planted in the bottom, rise all the way to the top, sway slightly in the movement of the water. Usually, they have one long vertical stalk, and branching out from that stalk are delicious leaves the fish and snails like to eat.

Now I want you to watch this aquarium. Get ready. Because if you watch long enough, you'll see a fish come over to the plant and take a little nibble off one of the leaves. It doesn't eat much, just a little bit. After taking a little nibble, that fish says, "Man, that was good!" And it swims away.

The fish swims around awhile and starts talking to the other fish. "You wouldn't believe what's over there in that corner. It's a plant. No, it's more than a plant. It's a salad bar! And it's free! And man, those leaves are good!"

And so the other fish have a little committee meeting and decide, "Why not? Let's give it a try." So over the next few days, other fish swim over to the plant and take a nibble. Some go back for seconds, but all the fish agree, "This plant is incredibly delicious!" And this little floating smorgasbord is great for the fish!

At least for a while.

And I say for a while because even though the fish are having the time of their lives, the plant is now having some problems. The fish are eating the leaves faster than the plant can grow them. The plant begins thinking to herself, "Boy, I sure could use a little rest. All they do is keep nibbling away at me. Why don't they give me a break? Don't they know it takes time to grow leaves? What do they think I am, a machine? I'm a plant! I can't produce leaves instantaneously." But no matter how much she says it, the fish seemingly just keeping nibbling and eating and munching away. They love the plant!

And then the moment of truth comes. The plant wakes up one morning, she looks in the mirror so she can comb her leaves, wants to make herself beautiful for the day as she usually does, but guess what? She has no more leaves. She has become a long, vertical, pencil-thin stalk of nothing—no longer good for the fish, no longer good to herself. She weeps in front of the mirror. "Look at me! Just look at me!" She just weeps in front of the mirror.

Do you ever feel like that plant?

The housewife who changes diapers day after day, who runs the kids here and there without even so much as a thank-you, who grocery shops but only hears complaints like "There's nothing to eat around here," who tries to make sure the house is clean, the home organized. Do you think she ever feels like all the leaves of her life have been nibbled away?

Or the executive who looks like he has it all with the nice salary and stock options and benefits. But do you think after a day of meetings and crises and decisions and demands on his time and expertise that he ever feels that all the leaves of his soul have been nibbled away?

And what about that sixteen-year-old who gets pressure to make the right grades, to do the right activities, to achieve so that she can get into the right school, find the right job, and she's got to find the right job so she can make the right kind of money. What about that pressure? Do you think that she ever feels as if the world is nibbling away on her life?

It's not easy to hang on to our lives, is it? I believe that God created each of us with the capacity to grow and flourish, to enjoy life and contribute to the lives of others. Each of us has that marvelous potential as human beings. In fact, one of the most sacred callings we have as Christians is to become as fully as possible what God created us to be. The problem, however, is that the world starts nibbling away at us. And that's why there are times when we must relentlessly, tenaciously, fiercely pursue the life God wants us to live.

And that's why I like this story about the Canaanite woman in the Gospel of Matthew. Here was a woman who had so much eating away at her life. For one thing, she was a woman in a male-dominated, chauvinistic society. That will eat away at you. Second, she was a non-Jew and, therefore, would not normally be accepted in the little circle of Jesus' followers. Exclusion will eat away at you. Third, she had a daughter who was very ill; consequently, she faced the terror of losing her own child. That kind of fear will eat away at you. The truth is, if this nameless woman had been a plant in an aquarium, I doubt if she would have had many leaves left on the stalk of her life.

Yet, notice what happens. Her desperation becomes, not despair, but determination. That's a sign of faith. She moves toward Jesus of Nazareth with her plea, "Please help my daughter!" Do you see that the very articulation of this need for her life required immeasurable courage? Women on the street just didn't talk to men like that; it was improper. Non-Jews just didn't talk to Jews like that; it was unacceptable.

Notice that the disciples try to shoo her away like a pesky fly at a picnic. And even Jesus, even Jesus, so focused on his mission to fellow Jews, says to the woman, "I've only come to help the lost sheep of Israel."

But this tenacious, relentless, leafless woman would not give up. She's trying to preserve a life. Her life. Her daughter's life. She falls down to her knees on that dusty road and says it as plainly as she can, "Lord, help me."

Jesus then uses a proverb, a cliche really, that circulated in the first century. He says, "It's not fair to take children's food and give it to the dogs." Sounds a little harsh, doesn't it? You see, Jesus is really quoting a saying that existed in the first century, the point of which is that priorities should be established and that, for him—since he was a Jew—his priority was to help fellow Jews in their religious life. It's not that he thought non-Jews were dogs; it's just that he knew that one person couldn't realistically reach everyone. Even saying all that, that cliche had to have cut to the feeling center of this woman.

And then the crucial moment. The woman came back with an expression of faith and courage and exhibited what Jews sometimes call "chutzpa." She said, "Yes, Lord, but even dogs get crumbs that fall from the table."

Amazing! In that one line there is courage and wit and humor and insight and faith. Imagine for a minute how easy it would have been for this woman to have said to herself, "Go ahead, world, nibble away. You've been eating me alive for years. Finish me off!" It would have been so easy for her to settle in with defeat and despair. It would have been so easy to have given up her dreams. After all, let's face it—despair is easier than determination. Oh, she could have become so comfortable with the "status-quo," with the "way-it's-always-been," with the "some-things-will-never-change" attitude. And we all do it. We all do it, not because we necessarily want to, but because we lack the imagination or the courage to say to the fish swimming around our lives, "You can have some of my leaves, but you cannot have all of my leaves."

And that's exactly what this remarkable woman did. She knew she had to preserve her life. And so she did. She moved toward Jesus Christ, even when everything was telling her to stay away. And she did not give up, even when all the signs said to give up. And the persistence she exhibited didn't so much earn her daughter's healing as it opened the door for it to happen.

And I think that's the point of the story—to be the people God wants us to be, sometimes, requires of us a fierce, tenacious, "never-give-up" kind of faith.

So, think about your life today. Is there some part of you that you've lost? Has some *cynicism* nibbled away at your hopefulness? Has some *routine* eaten away at your creativity? Has some *bitterness* replaced your God-created sweetness? Has some *despair* taken over where once there was determination? Has some kind of *pessimism* squeezed the life out of your optimism? Has some *selfishness* devoured your higher impulse to serve, to give, to help?

Henry James put it like this: "Live all you can; it's a mistake not to. It doesn't matter what you do in particular, so long as you have your life. If you haven't had that, what have you had?"

And that's exactly what this woman in our story sought from Jesus. She wanted to hang on to her life! And God created me and you not only to get a life, but to hang on to our life. Some have suggested that we live in an age of narcissism. And maybe that's true. But it's also true that we live in an age when people are living and working to the point of stress and sickness and disease. In fact, as one article in the *New York Times* recently pointed out, "People are working more because going home is so stressful. What once was a place of rest has become a place of stress." At some point we must learn that to balance life and take care of our lives is not narcissistic; it's living to the glory of God.

Winston Churchill was invited to give the commencement address at one of the colleges in Cambridge University several years ago. You can imagine the anticipation of the graduates, the honor they felt having this great world leader speak at the ceremony. The hall was filled to capacity. A buzz was in the air. And then Churchill's large presence walked across the stage. He moved to the lectern. Quiet descended upon the crowd. Churchill slowly scanned the young, eager faces of the graduates and said to them, "Don't give up."

And then he sat down. People didn't know what to do. Should we applaud? Is this it? A minute later he got up again, went to the lectern, and said, "Don't ever give up!" He sat down once more. Again, nothing but uncomfortable silence.

A third time he went to the lectern, looked at the crowd with those intense little eyes, and said, "Don't ever, ever, give up!" And then he walked offstage.

Folks, the fish swim all around us. A bite here. A nibble there. But God created you to grow and thrive; not just survive, but thrive. To be nourished by the goodness of life, and to nourish goodness in others. We glorify God by saving the world. But we also glorify God by enjoying the world. Be what God wants you to be. Hang on to your life. Find the tenacity you need to live your dreams. And most of all, don't give up!

Questions for Reflection

1. What is one part of your life you would like to reclaim for your own well-being and enjoyment?

2. Could you relate to the metaphor of the plant being nibbled to death? How might you set better boundaries so you can both give and re-plenish your life energy?

3. Look back on your life this past month, and name one experience that really gave you energy. If you're in a group, are there similar experiences? What do these experiences teach you about living life?

23

How Do I Know
I'm Really a Christian?

Scripture Text—1 John 3:18–24

*Little children, let us love, not in word or speech, but in truth and action. And
by this we will know that we are from the truth and will reassure our hearts before
him whenever our hearts condemn us; for God is greater than our hearts, and he
knows everything. Beloved, if our hearts do not condemn us, we have boldness before
God; and we receive from him whatever we ask, because we obey his commandments
and do what pleases him. And this is his commandment, that we should believe in
the name of his Son Jesus Christ and love one another, just as he has commanded
us. All who obey his commandments abide in him, and he abides in them. And by
this we know that he abides in us, by the Spirit that he has given us.*

Biblical Reflections

You don't often hear readings in church from the letters of John. The
books are either so personal that there's little to apply to our contemporary situation, or the theological thought processes are so dense and con-
voluted that it's hard to make sense of the argument. Yet, as I wanted to
preach a sermon on Christian confidence and assurance, this reading
seemed to fit perfectly.

You cannot imagine the number of Christians I've met through the
years who worry that "they won't go to heaven" or that "they aren't good
enough." Such worry, along with the riddled lives that worry creates, is
absolutely useless, and so unnecessary. I can easily say that, but I know

from personal experience that it's harder to live than say. Too often we try to live up to impossible standards. Thankfully, being a Christian is not really about living up to standards. It's about accepting the gift of God's grace and love.

In this sermon I try to help people understand that our salvation is not based upon our mood or the mood of God. Our assurance is rooted and grounded in the story of Jesus Christ, who reveals a God of unconditional love and acceptance, and which is finally never changing. There's really no need to ride the roller coaster of spiritual self-doubt. The heart of God assures us that we belong to God even when we can't find a way to assure ourselves. Now, that's something you can count on!

Sermon Text

Last fall, Dr. Kathleen Brandt was walking home from her job at New York's Institute of Fine Arts. On her way home, she passed by the French Embassy's cultural center on Fifth Avenue, a place she had walked past literally hundreds of times before. This time, however, the large, beautiful mansion was ablaze with light. People filled the lovely rooms as they mingled with cocktails and food, laughing, talking, enjoying the reception.

But as she walked past, she noticed through a window a three-foot statue of Cupid atop an interior courtyard fountain. It intrigued her. So interested was she that she actually walked through some shrubs and pressed her nose to the window to get a better look at this marvelous-looking statue. She noticed the delicately carved lines, the shadows, the muscles of the figure. She also noted the curls of the hair, the strap holding the quiver with arrows to the body. As she looked at the statue, her heart began to race.

The next day she received permission to examine the sculpture. She took with her a graduate assistant. For hours and then days, they examined the fascinating statue. Finally, she released the findings of her research and announced to the world that what she had discovered was actually an original sculpture of Michelangelo.

What's so ironic about the story is that this statue, located near the Metropolitan Museum of Art and in the heart of art scholarship, had been unnoticed for years. This artistic treasure had been there for nearly a century and no one, not even those living in the French Embassy, had even noticed it.

Do you think it could be that God is the unnoticed treasure of our lives? That our capacity to be in spiritual relationship with God is both our greatest gift and our most ignored potential? Do you think the soulful call to depth that makes us human is our most neglected masterpiece?

There's a little line in this reading from the letter of First John that I find fascinating. John encourages the Christians—he calls them "little children"—to love one another. That isn't merely talking about loving one another. That's not just conceptually believing in loving one another. John really expects them to love one another "in truth and action." And I like to think of truth as authenticity. The practice of being a Christian is to be authentic or real in relationship to others.

Now, I don't think John is talking about some attempt to earn salvation or to achieve God. None of us can do that. And if we try, we're either going to dive into despair or ascend into self-righteousness, neither of which is particularly attractive or pleasing to God.

I do think, however, that John means that there are certain practices that identify our lives as Christians. These practices proclaim that this is who we are, this is what we do, this is what we confess. Our practice of worship or our practice of service or our practice of authentic relationships—these practices define our Christian life. And John's point is, if we do these practices, then that will assure our hearts before God that we really are Christians.

Yet, what I find so interesting here is that John seems to know that there are moments in the Christian experience when we have self-inflicted and stabbing self-doubts. Moments when as Christians we wonder, "Am I *really* a Christian?" "Is God *really* with me?" And, yes, sometimes we even wonder, "If I were to die today, would I *really* spend eternity with God?" John acknowledges that doubting dimension of life when he says, "Whenever our hearts condemn us." What a powerful line. "Whenever our hearts condemn us." And they do, don't they? These hearts of ours, sometimes they do condemn us. Cold. Harsh. Unrelenting. And I don't know about you, but what I've found to be true in my own experience is that my heart wants to condemn me most at two critical moments of my living. One is when I've done something wrong, and the other is when I don't feel like I've done enough. .

To say that we all do things that are wrong is to state the obvious. But more than any wrong we do, what's most important is what we do after the wrong. Frequently, many of us follow up our mistake, not with ownership and responsibility, but with defensiveness and blame. That is, rather than facing the wrong we've done—confessing it, dealing with it—we try to either escape it or defend it.

One place in the Bible where you see people really facing the mistakes of their lives is in the book of Psalms. In those psalms, you find startling confession and honest admission of wrong done. You find writers saying things like, "Even my very bones are wasting away!" And that's what happens when we don't face our mistakes and failures; we internally waste away. And that's what happens to a society too. If we as citizens in the nation and world don't take responsibility for wrongs, then as a society we merely waste away. It's far too easy to blame the government. Too easy to blame the minorities. Too easy to blame the majorities. Too easy to blame labor. Too easy to blame management. It's too easy to blame the poor. Too easy to blame the rich. Because just as our souls only improve when we can own up to our own mistakes, society only improves when we can own up to our complicity in social wrongs.

But there's something else that happens when we do something wrong. Yes, sometimes we want to blame and defend. But most of the time after I do something wrong, my heart jumps to a big conclusion and begins saying, "You messed up big time, Colglazier!" (I don't know about you, but when my heart condemns me, it always uses my last name—like a tough coach or a mean professor.) "Colglazier, you really messed up big time!" And then my condemning heart takes a gargantuan leap and says, "And that means you are a big mess up!"

Do you hear how perniciously sinister that sounds? It's one thing to recognize that you have made a mistake, but it's completely another to begin believing that you are a mistake. Wrongs? We all do wrongs. But just because you've done something wrong doesn't mean that it's wrong for you to be in this world. Moreover, the temptation after every mistake we make—at home, in business, at church—is to sulk about it, brood over it, internalize it, overidentify with it, become chained to it. But that kind of response to our human mistakes is finally a waste of the beauty and poetry of the human spirit.

I have a friend who about three years ago went through a traumatic divorce. Before that, she was one of those people who was forever brimming over with confidence and joy. People just liked to be around her. But after that divorce something happened to her. Instead of recognizing either the mistake of the marriage or the mistakes that led to the divorce, she began internalizing all the failures of the relationship, and she started feeling like a mistake herself. Her problem was not that she blamed others; her problem was that she blamed herself to the point that she lost the sparkle of her self-esteem and the radiance of her confidence. Rather than saying, "This marriage was an honest mistake," she could only feel that "I am the mistake."

It's never a question of whether or not wrongs or failures will happen. They happen all the time, and they happen to all of us. The real question becomes What will we do with those moments when, after the mistake, our heart tries to condemn us? But there's another experience that I need to mention this morning, because it's even worse than dealing with wrongs we've done. It's this condemning feeling some of us live with that we're not adequate, not good enough, not doing enough as Christians. And if you've ever been there, you know what a private little hell inadequacy can become.

For some, not all, but for some, their entire orientation to being a Christian is this experience of inadequacy. "Are you a Christian?" "Well, I guess so" goes the answer. Or "I hope so" is the reply. Or even less enthusiastically, "I try to go to church." It's a low-grade guilt or shame that settles in the soul like California fog, so we're not really enjoying the Christian faith, not really living it up as a Christian, not really reaching out and making a positive difference in the world. Religion becomes more a source of our inadequacy than of our creative potency.

Now, I'll tell you when I really see this. On Sunday afternoons, if I'm out doing something and I happen to run into a member of University Christian and by some freak of nature they missed church that morning, you would think my name is Doctor Reverend Guilt! I mean, before I even say, "Hello," the wheels and words fly furiously. "Oh, I'm sorry, we weren't in church this morning. We've been so busy. Our daughter had a soccer game. It was so nice out we decided to play golf this morning. Oh, but don't worry, we'll be back next Sunday. No, we've got to go out of town next week, but we'll see you on Easter. We promise." I don't have the heart to tell them that I was sure I had seen them that morning in the balcony at eleven!

It's true that we all need to grow in our Christian faith, but as we grow we need to let go of the self-condemnation of not attending enough or not doing enough or not giving enough or not feeling enough. That kind of self-loathing runs against everything Jesus was about. If anything, the ministry of Jesus touched most profoundly the people who didn't feel worthy of being touched at all. Why do you think the drunks and the lepers and the prostitutes found him so compelling? It was because in him they found the key to unlock the door of their own little prison of not being good enough. In the first century Jesus was a symbol of hope; many of us at the end of the twentieth century have turned him into a symbol of guilt.

And I'll tell you what else is fascinating. Not only do we not feel good enough in our faith, but many of us also condemn ourselves in other areas of our lives. We feel bad for not having published as much as our colleagues. Or we beat up on ourselves for not being as successful as a sibling. Or we feel bad about ourselves for not having the physical bodies we would like to have. Or we feel that all the other parents are so much better than we are. Or we lack so much confidence that we assume that any man or any woman would be a better spouse or lover or provider than we are. Do you see how debilitating it is to live with a feeling that "I am not enough"?

John acknowledges the reality of self-condemnation in human experience. But then he offers the treasure. He says, "God is greater than our hearts." "God is greater than our hearts." Which is to say, when we can hardly live with ourselves, God still lives with us. And when we can no longer love ourselves, God still loves us. And when we want to give up on our lives, God hangs on that much tighter. And when we can't seem to forgive what we've done—and, believe me, forgiving ourselves is often harder than forgiving others—God still forgives us. To say that "God is greater than our hearts" is to say that divine love given to us in Jesus Christ is what *really* makes us Christians. We're not Christians because of how much we know or how much we do or even how much we feel. And we're not Christians because of how well we live up to a system of religion we call Christianity. We're Christians because of how much God loves.

And that, my friends—the truth of divine love—is like a priceless treasure. When you do things that are wrong, when you don't feel that you're enough, press your nose to the window. The lights are on. There's a big party. Go ahead. Look inside. It's like a discovered sculpture by Michelangelo that's been in the mansion of your heart all along.

Questions for Reflection

1. Have you ever doubted your own salvation or spiritual value before God?

2. When in your life experience do you experience self-condemnation?

3. Why do we condemn ourselves? How can we help others find greater self-esteem and confidence for living?

24

Falling in Love to Growing in Love

Scripture Text—1 Corinthians 13:1–8

If I speak in the tongues of mortals and of angels, but do not have love, I am a noisy gong or a clanging cymbal. And if I have prophetic powers, and understand all mysteries and all knowledge, and if I have all faith, so as to remove mountains, but do not have love, I am nothing. If I give away all my possessions, and if I hand over my body so that I may boast, but do not have love, I gain nothing. Love is patient; love is kind; love is not envious or boastful or arrogant or rude. It does not insist on its own way; it is not irritable or resentful; it does not rejoice in wrongdoing, but rejoices in the truth. It bears all things, believes all things, hopes all things, endures all things. Love never ends. But as for prophecies, they will come to an end; as for tongues, they will cease; as for knowledge, it will come to an end.

Biblical Reflections

I have read this particular scripture at hundreds of weddings throughout my years as a minister. Even though Paul was not addressing the topic of marriage in 1 Corinthians 13, it is certainly fitting for the context of weddings and marriage. That's why I selected it for this sermon.

This chapter thirteen of 1 Corinthians is actually part of three chapters that deal with specific problems in the worship service at Corinth. There were people being rude, disruptive, trying to outshine, outdo, outperform others in the church. Paul writes to help them see that there is a variety of

160

spiritual gifts, but the same God inspires the many gifts. Additionally, he tries to drive home the point that to have a spiritual gift requires love and compassion.

Although his message was for the church, his words have a way of speaking to love relationships too. In this sermon, I offer some reflections on love and relationships, trying to move people to a place of mature responsibility rather than immature fantasy that characterizes many contemporary marriages. Relationships continue to be the crucible in which many of our spiritual lives are formed. In our relationships of love we touch the mystery of the divine. This, of course, is why they are so glorious and maddening.

Sermon Text

The first time Marti and I stepped into the sanctuary of our church, she made a curious comment. She did not say how beautiful the sanctuary was or that she could imagine my preaching from the pulpit. Instead, she walked down the center aisle and simply said, "I can see Katie getting married here!" What made me nervous was when she said, "Why, I can see me getting married again here!"

Weddings do capture our fairy-tale imagination. The bride and groom become prince and princess. A wedding is Camelot. The flowers, the music, the candles, the tuxedos, the white wedding dress—it is all one package of fantasy. Let's see a show of hands this morning. How many of you had tears in your eyes when you watched Steve Martin in the movie *Father of the Bride?* Weddings are romantic, sentimental, emotional, and absolutely wonderful. But weddings are not marriages, and that is both good news and bad news for a lot of couples.

Weddings are about falling in love. Couples come into my office ready to get married, and I feel sometimes that I'm trying to rescue two people who are free floating in space like astronauts. I'm mission control trying to reach this couple orbiting around the church in their fantasy world.

I try to ask real, earthly, relationship questions like, "How long have you two known each other?" And they look into each other's eyes and give me some goofy answer like, "It feels like we've known each other forever!" That's not what I meant. So I try again. "Where do you plan to live after you get married?" And the bride says, "It doesn't matter where we live as long as I'm with him!" It's sick, I tell you, it's sick! I try again. "What about the wedding itself? What kind of wedding would you like?" The groom looks over at the bride and says with eyes as sincere as a Labrador retriever, "Whatever she wants is fine with me."

At this point, she is probably assuming that this is the way marriage is going to be. She doesn't realize that this man who just said, "Whatever she wants…" has just reached his life courtesy peak. It will not get any better than this! And he doesn't realize that his bride will never look better, shine brighter, be more radiant than she does right now! Both of them are living in a sparkled, spangled world of illusion!

Most romances begin this way. We fall in love. We use superlative language like "She is the most beautiful person in the world." "He is the most handsome man I've ever met." "She is the smartest woman I've ever been around." "He's more sensitive than any man I've ever dated." This is the language of idealization. This is the language of romance. And when we are having those feelings, it's like the rational part of our brain shuts down, and all we want to do is feel, feel, feel, and feel some more! And we want to feel because there is no more delicious feeling in the world than falling in love. When you are failing in love, it doesn't matter that you don't have enough money for a McDonald's cheeseburger. It doesn't matter that he loves riding Harley-Davison motorcycles and she likes playing genteel tennis with the girls at the club. None of it really matters because you are in love.

This first stage of love might be called the sparkle stage or the speed-ing stage or the stage of illusionment. Is this a bad stage? No. It's a won-derful stage. In fact, I think one reason this stage is so powerful is because it is for us a moment of divine transcendence. When we have this stage of idealization, it puts us in touch with the energy of God. We feel the other person to be God-like. So this stage is a wonderful stage. But after the wedding, something begins to happen. Suddenly, Prince Charming, you discover, leaves his dirty underwear on the bathroom floor. The prince that you married leaves wet towels on the bed in the mornings after his shower. The prince has annoying habits like coming home late and not calling, like smacking his lips at the dinner table while he eats. You didn't notice this while you were in the sparkle stage, but now, getting deep into the heavy industry of marriage, you begin to notice things.

And as for the princess. She doesn't always look radiant in the morn-ing when she first gets up. In fact, she's downright scary! And instead of wearing a lovely white wedding gown, do you know what she wears half the time around the house? Sweatpants! Folks, there are no secrets in sweatpants. I don't mean a nice warm-up mind you, but sweatpants and a T-shirt. And she has her habits, too. Prince Charming has noticed that the princess can be very stubborn. Sometimes the princess can hound and harangue like a drill sergeant.

And with these kinds of awarenesses, the marriage begins to move to a new stage. No longer in the stage of illusionment, the marriage has now started the stage of disillusionment. Idealizations, once so strong, now begin to shatter like a light bulb dropped on concrete. Bliss becomes pain. Heaven becomes hell. Happiness becomes misery. And the language changes dramatically.

Instead of the language of romance, we start to hear the language of human reality. "He doesn't talk to me anymore." "She doesn't fulfill my needs anymore." "He doesn't love me anymore." "She's always nagging." "He's always criticizing." "He's always blaming me." "She's always spending too much money." "He doesn't make enough money." And the one you hear all the time, "We've just drifted apart."

The psychologist Carl Jung once wrote, "Seldom or never does a marriage develop smoothly without a crisis. There is no birth of consciousness without pain." Listen to that. That's the most important line in this sermon: *There is no birth of consciousness without pain!*

You see, we have little relationship consciousness at the beginning. We're using all our energy to project all our idealizations upon our partner. But after a while, pain does come. The relationship begins breaking down. Now, for some couples, this breakdown is severe and traumatic. For others, the pain of this stage is gradual and annoying like a low-grade fever. But one thing is for sure, the world of the relationship changes after the initial stage of idealizing draws to a close.

What I want to say to you this morning is that the movement into this stage of disillusionment is not only necessary, but it is also good. You've heard the expression, "No pain, no gain!" Well, that is true of marriage. It seems to me that as couples we really have three options with this stage of marital disillusionment.

One option is that we can simply deny that there is pain in the marriage. The pain is there, but this little voice inside our head says, "Oh, it's not that bad. Just ignore it. It will go away. Nobody's perfect. Grin and bear it. Be a good boy. Be a good girl." But let me tell you what I've experienced. Every feeling I've tried to pretend was not there has always, I mean always, come back to haunt me like a demon. When we don't deal with feelings, they herniate somewhere else in our lives. So, when we don't deal with the pain of the marriage, it herniates in the form of pain with our children. Rather than deal with the pain of the relationship, we project our pain on the people with whom we work. We can try to deny pain, but pain always comes back to hit us in the head like a boomerang.

Another option is that we can divorce. Not deny, but divorce. The idealizations gone, the illusions punctured, we feel the marriage crack like ice underneath our feet, and we assume that we must have married the wrong person, that something is wrong with the marriage, that there is probably somebody out there who can do a better job at making us happy.

We're not really sure why the magic of the marriage has been lost, but we assume that if there is marital pain, then that is a sign that the marriage is over. And I don't have to tell you that over fifty percent of all couples who are married finally choose this option.

But the trouble with divorce is that rarely are you trading misery for bliss. Instead, divorce has its own form of misery. Many of you know that firsthand. There is emotional devastation. There is family trauma. There is social estrangement. There is financial depletion. All of that is pain! Now, there are some marriages that need to come to an end because they finally have lost all potential to enhance life, which is why God gave us marriage in the first place. But, for the most part, after a divorce everyone comes out a loser. I admire those people who have gone through the pain of a divorce and have rebuilt their lives. It is not easy because divorce is painful.

But there's another option, and that is the option of development. Not denial of pain. Not divorce from pain. But development from pain. What I mean is that relationship pain is not a sign that the marriage should be thrown away, but it's a sign of a new kind of relationship's trying to be born. There is no birth without pain. There is no new life without the discomfort of skin being stretched and pulled. There is no growth without the aches and pains of our marital bones.

This is why when couples say to me, "We're just not getting along anymore. She's not the way she used to be. He's not the same person I married. We've changed through the years," I want to get up and hug both of them and say, "Isn't it absolutely fantastic that you are in so much pain? God's about ready to give birth to a new depth of relationship!" It can happen. But you have to hang in there with each other, and you have to make a commitment to grow.

Marriages can move from the stage of illusionment to the stage of disillusionment to a third stage that I would call the relational depth stage. In the depth stage, the partners have grown together. They have become life partners in the deepest sense of that word. They aren't dependent on each other as much as they are interdependent with one another. Both have become full human beings in their own right. They bring to the marriage the fullness of who they are, not just their emptiness. They are not saviors to one another. They are not happy machines for each other. Instead, they live in the growing partnership of love.

Isn't it ironic that this reading from 1 Corinthians 13, a reading that really portrays an amazing depth of love, is always read at a wedding, the highest moment of human idealization? Paul's words are not romantic. They are practical, hard, demanding words.

"You mean, Paul, love is not just a feeling? You mean love is not keeping score? You mean love is not bringing up the past and throwing it in my partner's face? You mean love is not treating our partner as an irritation at the end of the day? You mean to tell me, Paul, that love is resisting marital put-downs, resisting making myself look better than my spouse? You mean to tell me that God really expects me to practice the art of believing the best in my spouse, of not waiting for a mistake that can be blown up and blame placed?" "Yes," Paul would say, "the Word of God does mean to tell us that!"

So how does a couple move into that kind of relationship depth? Let me offer a couple of suggestions that might be helpful.

First of all, accept the difficulty of creating a good marriage. Marriage is not easy. There is no magical partner out there who is going to make your life better. Good marriages take time. They take effort. They take energy. They take learning new skills. They take the deepest of our human feelings. I know, I saw *Sleepless in Seattle,* too. And I like the idea that there just might be the perfect woman waiting for me at the top of the Empire State Building on Valentine's Day. I like the idea of that, but I also know that dreaming of romance is no substitute for accepting the fact that good relationships require hard work.

Second, learn to embrace the dark side of your own personality. Now, you may be thinking, there's nothing wrong with my personality. It's all her fault. It's all his fault. But the truth is it can be a great breakthrough when a husband can say to his wife, "I know that I tend to be too critical. I know I tend to be too controlling. I know that I tend to be too judgmental." And marriages can move to a new stage of depth when the wife can say, "I know that I tend to be too possessive. I know I tend to be too concerned about appearances. I know that I tend to be too set in my ways." What happens many times in our marriages is that rather than owning up to that which is negative in our own lives, we tend to stick our negative traits on the Velcro of our spouse. And believe me, blame takes relationships nowhere!

Third, intentionally develop friendship in your marriage. I think one of the highest compliments that any spouse can pay his or her mate is this: "He or she is my best friend." I see this in marriages in our church that seem to have longevity and happiness. These couples have found ways to become good company with each other. They have discovered activities with each other that are fun and playful. They have learned how to have meaningful conversations with each other. What happens for many of us is that we forget to attend to that which is most lasting in the marriage, namely friendship. Our physical potency will decline. Our appearances will diminish. Our children will grow up and move away. But it is this gift of marital friendship that finally gives life depth. Make the effort, give the time, share the emotion, and be friends.

Fourth, practice loving behaviors in the marriage. I know that seems like such a simple thing to say, but what happens in our disillusionment stage is that we start practicing all kinds of destructive behaviors in the relationship. We do this because we are in pain. But the behaviors become self-destructive. We withhold affection. We give the deep freeze. We yell and intimidate. We manipulate the children to be on our side. We pout. We get angry. We leave the house. We emotionally attack. We blame. Now, I know that it embarrasses us that we behave this way, but it is true. We all have behaved this way. We all have our relationship weapons. But when a couple moves toward depth they begin choosing loving behaviors. Instead of advising, for example, we learn to listen. Instead of pouting, we learn to share our feelings. Instead of blaming, we learn to accept responsibility. Instead of taking for granted, we learn to express our gratitude. Loving behaviors may not be easy to learn, but if we practice this kind of love, then our life is filled with love.

And fifth, embrace the spiritual journey of the marriage. What I find to be true is that the very issues in my relationship with Marti are the same issues in my relationship with God. The need to listen is not only true of my marriage, it is also true of my relationship with Jesus Christ. My need to be more grateful is just as true of my spiritual life as it is true of my family life. What I really want to say is that marriage can be a soulful experience. Do you know what a sacrament is? A sacrament is one of the rituals of the church that people do in order to receive the presence of God. Therefore, communion is a sacrament. When we eat bread and drink from the cup, we then experience God's companionship. Baptism is a sacrament. When we are baptized, we experience the presence of God through that ritual of washing. I think marriages, too, can be a sacrament. Through taking care of daily life together, growing together, serving together, paying bills together, buying groceries and furniture together, talking together, touching one another, I think we can experience the presence of God.

I hope for all of you this morning that you can find a way to move from falling in love to growing in love. Relationships may begin in Camelot and endure some pain in hell. But if the commitment to grow and deepen is there, what might be possible is that best stage of loving—the stage of depth. It's the kind of love found in 1 Corinthians 13. It is only in that stage that it can be said, "Love never ends."

Questions for Reflection

1. Can you remember the first time you fell in love? What was it like?

2. Can you recall a time when you were first disillusioned in a relationship?

3. What is the one thing you could do to help deepen your most intimate relationship?